S0-APN-902

THE

Newsletter

Editor's

DESK BOOK

MARVIN ARTH, HELEN ASHMORE & ELAINE FLOYD

4th Edition

NEWSLETTER
resources

Other publications from Newsletter Resources:
Marketing With Newsletters
Making Money Writing Newsletters
101 Ways to Save Money on Newsletters
Quick & Easy Newsletters on a Shoestring Budget
Copy Ready Forms for Newsletters
Newsletter News & Resources

The Newsletter Editor's Desk Book: A concise review of journalism principles updated to include the editor's role in desktop publishing and publications management.

© 1980 by Marvin Arth and Helen Ashmore.
© 1981, 1984 by Parkway Press.
© 1995 by Marvin Arth, Helen Ashmore and Elaine Floyd.

All rights reserved. No part of this book may be reproduced in any form without the written consent of the publisher, except in the form of brief excerpts or quotations for the purposes of review.

Cataloging-in-Publication Data
Arth, Marvin.
    The newsletter editor's desk book : a concise review of journalism principles updated to include the editor's role in desktop publishing and publications management / Marvin Arth, Helen Ashmore & Elaine Floyd. — 4th ed.
    p. cm.
    Includes bibliographical references and index.
    ISBN 0-9630222-2-9

    1. Newsletters.   I. Ashmore, Helen.   II. Floyd, Elaine   III. Title.

PN4784.N5A78 1995   808'.06607
                                              94-21166

Fourth Edition. First Printing. Printed and bound in the United States.

Cover and page design: Kimberly DeRousse
Managing editor: Susan Todd

Newsletter Resources
6614 Pernod Avenue, St. Louis, MO 63139-2149
(314) 647-0400; FAX: (314) 647-1609

ISBN: 0-9630222-2-9   SAN: 297-4541

Distributed to the trade by Lifetime Books, Hollywood, FL (800) 771-3355

We dedicate this new edition
to our new additions,

Eliot Jack Guin
&
Danièle Rose Todorov.

Contents

PREFACE TO THE FOURTH EDITION XI

INTRODUCTION—HOW TO USE THIS BOOK ... 1

A Job Well Done, 3
Where to Start, 3
One Step at a Time, 4

1—SPREAD THE NEWS 7

The Private "Newspaper," 9
All Over the World, 9
All Shapes & Sizes, 9
The Editor's First Job, 10

2—WHO NEEDS A NEWSLETTER? 11

Do We Need a Newsletter?, 13
What Do We Expect From It?, 14
Keeping Readers, 15
Newsletters in the Public Relations Context, 17
The Newsletter That Is the Program, 17

3—MANAGEMENT SKILLS FOR EDITORS 19

Who's Going to Do What?, 21
Leadership Skills for Editors, 21
Building a Newsletter Team, 22
Finding & Motivating Volunteers, 23
Your Network of Reporters & Stringers, 28
Help From Outside Professionals, 30
Who's in Charge?, 31
The Boss Who Can't Let Go, 33
What Equipment is Available?, 34
In-House vs. Outside Page Layout, 35

4—TARGET THE NEWS 37

Is There News in a Newsletter?, *39*
Inside News Sources, *39*
Outside News Sources, *41*
Series & Features, *42*
The Multiple Audience Dilemma, *45*
What's News in Employee Publications, *46*
Finding the Right Tone, *47*
The External Newsletter, *49*
The Editor as Advocate, *49*

5—GATHER THE NEWS 53

Maintaining Journalistic Objectivity, *55*
Prime News Sources, *55*
Interviewing Like a Pro, *56*
Preparing Questions for the Interview, *57*
Doing Your Homework, *57*
Conducting the Interview, *58*
Keeping Good Files, *60*
Protecting Credibility, *60*
Watching for Legal Problems, *62*

6—PROFESSIONAL WRITING & EDITING .. 67

Selecting a News Style, *69*
Straight Reporting, *69*
Feature Treatment, *70*
Writing the Interview Story, *72*
The Essential Stylebook, *73*
Elements of News Writing, *75*
Writing Good Leads, *78*
Writing the Body, *81*
Making a Two-Story Story, *83*
7 Tips for Professional Speed, *85*
Rewriting a Story, *85*
Editors All Over the Place , *86*
A Checklist for Editors, *87*
Editing With Grammar Checkers, *88*

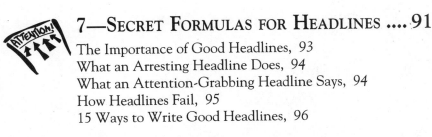

7—SECRET FORMULAS FOR HEADLINES 91

The Importance of Good Headlines, 93
What an Arresting Headline Does, 94
What an Attention-Grabbing Headline Says, 94
How Headlines Fail, 95
15 Ways to Write Good Headlines, 96

8—EDITING FOR DESIGN 101

Editing for Visually-Effective Design, 103
Letting Readers Come Up for Air, 103
Writing Kickers & Decks, 105
Creating Digestible Bites With Subheads, 106
Captivating Captions, 107
Principles of Pull Quotes, 108
Pulling in Readers With Teasers, 109

9—READER-FRIENDLY DESIGNS 111

Readability & the Right "Look," 113
Selecting Paper & Sizes, 113
Finding Legible Typefaces, 114
Matching Type Sizes to Audience, 116
Emphasizing With Type Styles, 117
Selecting a Typeface for Body Copy, 117
Establishing Headline Typefaces & Sizes, 120
The Word Processed Newsletter, 124
The Desktop Published Newsletter, 124
Finding the Ideal Line Length, 128
Plunging Into Picas, 129
When to Change Default Settings, 130
Copyfitting in the Electronic Age, 135
Counting Words for Articles, 135
Making Headlines Fit, 136
Avoiding 7 Design Culprits, 138
Learning by Doing, 142

10—LAYING OUT EACH ISSUE 143

Putting it All Together, *145*
Dummying Your Layout, *145*
Jumping Stories, *148*
Marking Specifications, *149*
Elements of Layout, *150*
Selecting the Best Photographs, *152*
Readying Photos for Layout, *156*
Dressing Up Pages, *159*

11—PRODUCTION & DISTRIBUTION 161

Preventive Care, *163*
What Do Good Proofreaders Do?, *163*
Cost-Effective Printing, *167*
Distributing Your News, *168*
Keeping Up With Your Mailing List, *168*
Mailing Through the Post Office, *169*

12—EDITORS OF THE FUTURE 171

From Desktop to Online, *173*
"Pull" vs. "Push" Communications, *173*
Good Journalism is Still Good Journalism, *174*

APPENDIX 1—PUBLICATION GUIDELINES ... 175

Mission Statement, *177*
Guidelines for Submitted Articles, *177*
Guidelines for Illustrations & Photographs, *178*
Layout Style Sheet, *178*

APPENDIX 2—MODEL STYLEBOOK 181

Punctuation, *183*
Capitalization, *188*
Spelling, *190*
Abbreviations, *194*
Numbers, *197*
Grammar, *199*

APPENDIX 3—FORMULA STORIES 211

Formulas Streamline the Routine, *213*
Personnel Items, *213*
Meetings, *214*
Speeches, *215*
Reports, *216*
Notices, *217*
Controversies, *218*

APPENDIX 4—FORM CONTRACTS 221

Vendor Contract, *223*
Print Purchase Agreement, *226*
Imagesetting Purchase Agreement, *227*
Mail House Purchase Agreement, *228*

APPENDIX 5—RESOURCES FOR EDITORS 229

Books & Booklets on Newsletters, *231*
Books on Design & Typography, *232*
Books on Photography, *233*
Books on Information Graphics, *233*
Books on Production, *234*
Publications on Design & Editing, *234*
Fillers for Newsletters, *235*
Clip Art Manufacturers, *236*
Cartoons, *237*
Newsletter Directories, *237*
Professional Associations, *238*
Writer's References, *239*
Newsletter Seminars, *240*
Writing & Interviewing Seminars, *240*
Calendar Making Software, *241*
Creativity Software, *241*
Online Research, *241*

INDEX 243

ABOUT THE AUTHORS & COLOPHON 251

Preface to the Fourth Edition

Since 1979, when the first edition of *The Newsletter Editor's Desk Book* was written, the world of newsletter publishing has undergone so radical a technological change as to be almost unrecognizable today. In the computer age, that world seems as extinct as the Tyrannosaurus Rex. Some few old dreamers like us remember with nostalgia the typewriters and paste-up boards of the valiant Human Age when newsletters were brought into the world by the laying on of hands streaked with rubber cement.

You will be astonished to learn—unless you are among them—that some people still write newsletter articles on typewriters. If you still write a newsletter on a typewriter, it still can be as good—and as readable—as any newsletter produced with all the latest desktop bells and whistles. The most important thing is still the news, and how the news is written.

That said, the fact is that the last typewriter will soon go the way of the quill pen and that we must bustle on to catch up with today's schoolchildren—most of whom are more computer-literate by the time they graduate than we will ever be.

And so the *Desk Book* enters the computer age reluctantly, yet profoundly mindful of the connection to the world that the computer so democratically offers. Not just the corporate or large association editor, but any editor in any room in any outpost (where an electric outlet or battery can be found) now can gather, write, and send forth news in flawless spell-checked pages—with dazzling facility and speed.

When the third edition of this book came out in 1984, we wrote that there was "little specific academic training" for newsletter editors. Since then, we have seen such training offered by high schools and colleges using this book as a text.

We wrote then of the hope that "this might become *the little book of newsletter editing*—that is, both the tidiest and the most respected reference on its subject, an asset to editors of every skill level." With 10,000 copies sold, and sales burbling along with no provocation or promotion on our part, the book did seem to have a life of its own.

But for all its virtue and tenacity, it was looking toward a rather quiet decline into old age until Elaine Floyd, a bright young star among newsletter pros, came along. She liked our book. We liked hers. The snappy excellence that jumped off the page at us when we first saw her *Marketing With Newsletters* now brings new life to the venerable *Newsletter Editor's Desk Book*. With this edition, Elaine brings us smartly into the desktop and onscreen publishing age.

Helen Ashmore & Marvin Arth
Boston & Kansas City
January 1, 1995

Introduction

How to Use This Book

Use this book so that it helps you with your own publication at your own pace.

A Job Well Done

Professional journalists are putting out thousands of good newsletters in this country. They know what they're doing, and this book will serve more to *remind* than to *inform* them.

There are also thousands of inexperienced editors of modest news publications that yield little compensation in worldly goods or glory. The volunteer publicity person for a special interest group or club, the association executive who is essentially a one-person staff, an assistant or secretary who is *volunteered* to do the company news—anyone around who looks able to do the job—may suddenly one day become a news editor.

These people are on the line. With little—sometimes no—journalistic training, they are expected to put out good newsletters, often in their "spare time" from a host of other pressing duties. It is for such editors that this book is primarily intended. We hope that it will enable them to resolve the many issues they face—or at least to know in concrete terms what the issues are—and to put out quality newsletters with a minimum of anxiety and a maximum of pleasure in a job well done.

Where to Start

If you edit a special-audience newsletter or newspaper, this book will help you. It does not matter if you are the most or least experienced journalist on earth, if you type the news yourself and hand it out to 30 Friends of the Teapot, or do International Marketing's *Customer News*—typeset and mailed to 250,000 people. A newsletter is a special form of communication and this is a special book jam-packed with information about that form.

If you are a novice editor, don't be intimidated by the many suggestions between these covers. Don't feel that in your first issue after you get the book you must suddenly do everything as well as a veteran newspaper editor does, according to the principles of classical journalism set forth here. Do what seems to you to be most important. Do things in order, for your readers.

Unless you have the skills and need to do an elaborate multi-column layout, skip the chapters on that subject, at least for now. If you put out a brightly written, cleanly produced *letter* with *news* in it, you'll have readers and you'll be serving them well. A *news letter* that is typed and looks like a letter conveys a personal feeling and an immediacy that typeset newsletters do not. Don't be ashamed to send out good typed newsletters. They work.

Trouble usually comes from single-spacing long and badly written stories, then sending out many crowded pages of these visual and intellectual offenses. The unhappy, would-be reader sinks into the mire. (If you use a one-column design, increase the left and right margins, double-space, use some underlining, write the news brightly and briefly, and limit the number of pages to two or three. This works just fine for Mr. Kiplinger—editor of the famous *Washington Kiplinger Letter*. It can work for you.)

No matter what your editing skills and ambitions, you will get the most out of this book if you first sit down with the last few issues of your newsletter, school newspaper, membership or other special-audience publication. Seriously gauge its strengths and weaknesses.

Is it interesting? Is it well-written? Is it accurate? Are facts and figures, including contact phone numbers and dates, times and locations of future events, *right?* How does it look? How are the headlines? *Give yourself a hearty pat on the back for its good points.* Then map out a plan to attack its failings, at a reasonable rate. Use this book, in other words, so that it helps you with your own publication and at your own pace.

ONE STEP AT A TIME

Set your pace based on your comfort level with computers, desktop publishing and other technology. Though it may seem overwhelming at first, computers *can* make your job as editor easier.

Desktop publishing places the entire management of the newsletter on the editor's shoulders. Go slowly and take along this book to help. Seek ways the computer can streamline rather than bottle-neck the production of your newsletter. Continue to learn about new time-saving electronic tools. Implement changes in a methodi-cal way, and your success as an effective editor and publications manager will be assured.

Chapter 1

Spread the News

*It's content that makes
a newsletter a newsletter.*

THE PRIVATE "NEWSPAPER"

Every business, association, school, church and club of any size at all in this country has a newsletter, a powerful indication that people like private news. A newsletter is a private, small-format newspaper that conveys specific information to a specific audience. It influences the reader's perception of the publishing organization, and anticipated reader response is assent or support in any form, from hard cash to increased loyalty or effort.

ALL OVER THE WORLD

Newsletters are being published all over the world—by everyone from powerful multinational corporations to scrappy entrepreneurs working alone at home. These publications differ greatly, therefore, in format, content, audience and purpose. School newspapers are in many respects newsletters.

Most newsletters are published monthly, some weekly or daily; some have no set frequency. Probably the most famous irregular frequency publication was written by the late Theodore Bernstein, assistant managing editor of *The New York Times*. His mimeographed letter identified the best and the worst headlines and story writing in that newspaper. "Winners and Sinners" was intended for internal circulation at *The Times* but gained an audience in newsrooms and journalism schools throughout the country. At the bottom of the letter was a notice, "W&S is issued occasionally from the southeast corner of *The New York Times* newsroom."

ALL SHAPES & SIZES

Newsletters may have 30 readers or 300,000. They may be written in conversational style or in formal prose. They have many purposes: to inform, persuade, promote, sell, reminisce, boost morale, educate, solicit money…or any combination of these.

Newsletters may be a single page or many pages. They vary in format from a tiny $4\,{}^1\!/_2$ x 6 inches to broadsheet (newspaper size) of 22 x 35 inches. Most, as the name implies, are letter-sized.

Some are so big and so expensively produced—four-color printing on glossy paper, with photographs, artwork, and elaborate typography—that people call them magazines. Most employee or association "magazines" are newsletters in fancy dress.

Some newsletters carry advertising, some charge subscription prices; but most are financed by their sponsors— banks, insurance companies, associations, cities, government agencies, schools, churches, unions, social clubs and entrepreneurs.

THE EDITOR'S FIRST JOB: DEFINING THE AUDIENCE

The newsletter editor must make many decisions about the format, layout, paper and the typeface that will best serve the publication's purpose. But *it is content that makes a newsletter a newsletter,* that sets it off from the general newspaper or the promotional advertising brochure. The newsletter falls somewhere between those two forms of communication. All newsletters involve gathering stories, writing and editing, copying and distributing, just as newspapers do. But, like advertising fliers, all are in one sense or another *selling something to their particular audience.*

The audience for most newsletters share a common interest: they all go to the same school, have money in the same bank, have Corvettes, served in the same military outfit, work at the same place or belong to the same club or church. A large company or professional association newsletter often addresses more than one public. Such a wide-audience publication is read by people with varying interests: employees or members and management, their families, stockholders, customers, the competition and other interested people.

Identifying readers for a newsletter is the editor's first job. Only when the editor does this job can the newsletter do its job—get the right message across to the right audience.

Chapter 2

Who Needs a Newsletter?

*It is said that to succeed
an organization should do the right thing
and let people know about it.*

Do We Need a Newsletter?

"Do we need a newsletter?" you rightfully ask. Publishing one on a regular basis can be time-consuming and costly. Could the time and money be better spent on other forms of communication? More frequent meetings, sales calls, fliers, a simple calendar of events? How about computer hookups, online information via an internal or external network? Local cable television? Could the target audience be reached more effectively by letters, telephone calls, fax or e-mail messages? Perhaps a combination of these approaches will serve your needs.

In many cases, however, a newsletter is the most effective and economical way to reach those you want to reach with the information you want them to have. If your group has grown so large that personal communication among its members has become unlikely, difficult or impossible, a newsletter can help overcome the problem. *A newsletter can provide a sense of continuity and community to an organization of any size or character.*

A newsletter is crucially important in the following instances:

- If readers are so scattered that close communication is difficult, a newsletter can provide a communicating link.
- If readers need certain detailed or technical information on a regular basis, a newsletter can provide it.
- If certain goals must be promoted among a group, a newsletter can examine and explain those goals to all the readers.
- If an organization depends on continuing contact with members or customers, a newsletter can remind them of the services provided by the organization.

A newsletter in these cases is the right medium for the message. When the mass media ignores a message because of its "limited audience" appeal, chances are that audience is properly a newsletter audience...that the newsletter *is the most efficient, economical way to reach them.*

WHAT DO WE EXPECT FROM IT?

Once it has been determined that the newsletter is the best way to get your news to your readers, the interested purpose the newsletter will serve (also called the mission) should be carefully considered. That purpose can be general or specific and need not be rigidly fixed. But it should be clear—clear enough to leave no room for doubt about what it is intended to accomplish. If you are uncertain, the newsletter will reflect this uncertainty.

These are examples of general purpose:

1. To improve image, attract money and generate support.
2. To motivate readers: improve employee morale, reward volunteers, increase productivity, attract new members, strengthen loyalties.

These are examples of specific purpose:

1. To advise members of a rural cooperative of energy savings techniques.
2. To attract customers to a bank savings plan—and keep them.

Sometimes newsletters have short-term goals. For example, the newsletter of a company going through a restructuring may have the short-term goal of shutting down the "rumor mill" by giving employees accurate, timely information.

An editor who understands the purpose of the newsletter does not have to agonize over questions involving content. Why should we run this story? What general or specific purpose does it serve? If, for instance, the main purpose of a newsletter is to sell new products to customers, then personal items about employees are probably out of place.

But if the purpose is to build employee morale, encourage camaraderie and open communications among a large staff—say in a metropolitan hospital—then personal items as well as stories about the superior services of the hospital are proper.

One purpose served by the newsletter, and of which editors do not always seem to be conscious, is that of projecting the image of the organization. What image do you wish to convey to your readers? Decide. (Decide with other people who have something to say about it—see *Who's in Charge?* in Chapter 3, page 31.)

A hospital employee relations department may wish to convey a sense of family and community, so it prints a colorful, chatty, casual publication that appeals to average employees, one that talks *about* and *to*, not *down to* them.

A government agency may wish to convey an image of economy to its taxpaying readers—they are, after all, footing the bill. So they print black on inexpensive white standard-size paper and avoid frills. The tone of the writing is professional; they wish to project competence, not frivolousness.

An investment firm wishes to project affluence, so it uses flashy artwork and color combinations, unusual paper size and texture to project unique success, to suggest to customers that this firm is indeed where all the right money is. A professional association that wishes to attract new members may use slick graphics and handsome paper to convey "prestige."

Editors of subscription newsletters want to establish credibility so readers will subscribe or renew. Their newsletters are packed with helpful information. Most subscription newsletter editors use simple designs that speed production. The result is that hot news lands in readers' hands quickly.

Keeping Readers

The wise editor keeps readers clearly in mind. Readers kept in mind are those who keep reading. Easy. But for some editors this isn't as easy as it may sound.

It is easy enough for the entrepreneur who edits and sells a newsletter on how to invest in gold coins. He probably works alone or with a very small staff. He has one audience—people who want to make money in gold. He has one purpose—to tell them how to do that. Pleasing board members, sales people or secretaries is not his goal.

At the other end of the spectrum is the editor of the large hospital or insurance company newsletter with multiple audiences to please. While all parties share a common interest in the organization's activities and well-being, each group has a specific interest. Hospital board members, for instance, want to see the bottom line figures from the annual report. Employees want to see themselves recognized for the hard work they do. The doctors like to see themselves receiving awards from professional associations.

An editor of such a multiple audience publication can clarify the picture by counting audiences—in a list. Who does it go to? Why? Who's more important than who in this lineup? The sales force? The clerical staff? The board? The clients? Which stories in the last newsletter were of interest to all parties? Which ones to one group only? *Is the newsletter written largely for one group at the expense of having the others become unhappy nonreaders?*

It is not always possible to satisfy widely different audiences with the same publication. Sometimes it becomes necessary to publish two newsletters—one internal, chiefly for employees or members, and one external, for the general public. Many large organizations do this. Employees or members receive both newsletters, but outsiders do not receive the insiders' newsletter.

The smaller the organization, the more likely it is that one newsletter will serve it. By the time it grows considerably, it will probably have two newsletters—the external one and a monthly, weekly or even, in some large companies, a daily news sheet telling what's for lunch and where to sign up for basketball tickets.

Many editors are able to reach a large section of their audience through e-mail or by fax. A newsletter transmitted this way can be highly effective since the time between the news being written and sent out is practically no time.

Newsletters in the Public Relations Context

It is said that *to succeed an organization should do the right thing and let people know about it.* Letting people know about it is a function of public relations.

A public relations department or person provides the mass media with news releases, texts of important speeches, notices of significant meetings and conventions, the results of those meetings, and notices of policy changes. The general public may be reached with this information via the annual report, public meetings and lectures by your organization's spokespersons.

Public relations people should cooperate, not put up barriers, in dealing with the mass media and the public at large, remembering, however, that their first obligation is always to the organization they serve. But the organization has a specific audience that cannot always be reached through the mass media.

It is reached through a newsletter.

The Newsletter That Is the Program

Newsletters that go to widely scattered readers who rarely see one another are crucial to the reader's perception of the publishing organization. They set the tone for, define the organization for subscribers or members. In fact, in a sense, such newsletters quite often *are* to readers the associations or businesses they represent—something they can hold in their hands, share with others. Thoughtful planning of these publications is, therefore, especially important. Be sure they project the image you want to project.

Chapter 3

Management Skills for Editors

Editors coordinate the skills of people both inside and outside of the organization...with the objective of creating a publication that everyone can be proud of.

WHO'S GOING TO DO WHAT?

Some editors—of major industry publications, for instance—are primarily top-level managers. They coordinate a team of professional writers, copy editors, photographers and graphic artists. They have sophisticated electronic publishing systems and help from commercial printers. Once the newsletter is printed, their mailing staff or service gets it out pronto.

Other editors have no such team. They are, what one editor calls, "A staff of one." The editor is also the writer, photographer, artist, desktop publisher, copier and mail clerk—and perhaps, the company owner.

This chapter is primarily for those editors who fall somewhere between these two extremes—who work for a middle-sized, perhaps growing, organization where some help is available from members or the staff and/or from contracted outside services.

In these organizations, many questions come up about who should do what to make the newsletter the best possible product at the lowest possible cost. The better editor is at coordinating available resources, the more enjoyable the project will be for everyone involved.

LEADERSHIP SKILLS FOR EDITORS

Most newsletter editors coordinate the skills of people both inside and outside of the organization—people from other departments, peers, bosses, outside vendors. Most editors are in unique positions because they have no direct authority to "manage" this staff. Instead, effective newsletters are managed through *leadership*.

The editor's objective is to build a team of reporters, writers, photographers and vendors and to coordinate all of these efforts to create a publication everyone is proud to be a part of.

Building a Newsletter Team

The first step in building a newsletter team is to first assess your own strengths and skills. Other publicity duties may be many, so you must determine how much time you can realistically devote to the newsletter. Then look around you to see where talented help may be available.

If the organization is large, or getting that way, it is probably impractical to track down every single news item yourself. Are there enough enthusiastic, bright people to make a reporter/stringer system feasible? Even within one building, *reporters* can be helpful in collecting routine information from their areas or departments, and they can relay tips for stories you might otherwise never hear of. If you have distant offices or chapters, *stringers* (off-site contributing reporters) can be invaluable in providing both routine information and occasional news tips and stories. Stringers keep you current with the big picture—the whole organization, not just your corner of it—an important asset for obvious reasons.

The speed of faxing and electronic mail makes a stringer system all the more appealing, for the time it takes to get the news sent across town or across the world now is no time. News sent via electronic mail on the Internet—including private commercial systems such as America Online, CompuServe and Prodigy—offer the editor the added benefit of already having the text keyed in.

Occasionally, stringers turn up who are talented enough to do more than gather news tips and routine information. They can also write the stories. As many college graduates in the 1980s were communications or marketing majors, it may not be hard to find some of them around—quite likely in jobs that do not tap into all that journalism training.

If, in your assessment of your own strengths and skills, you admit you really are not a good photographer, there's probably a talented photographer close by. Check office walls for good photographs, and ask who took them. If publication design isn't your strong suit, notice the layout of internal memos and fliers. Find out who's running the computer program that produced them.

Before you solicit the help of others, ask yourself a few questions. With an internal newsletter, ask: Will newsletter assignments bolster or burden staff already involved in other projects? Do they have time for them? Ask potential contributors. Ask their supervisors. Work with management to make the decision.

With an external customer, member or donor newsletter, the questions are: Do contributors understand the organization's marketing or fund-raising approach? Do they know how to attract your readers?

The question from the editor's point of view is: Will this person be more help than hindrance? *Decide before you ask for his or her help on the publication.*

Helping with the newsletter adds prestige and variety for someone whose position has become routine. People like to be published. It can boost morale to add people to your newsletter team.

FINDING & MOTIVATING VOLUNTEERS

Many an editor would welcome members to their newsletter staff, but volunteers are elusive. Finding and keeping good volunteers requires a system for coordinating their efforts. Volunteers resent having their time wasted. They will only let it happen once, and then they will disappear. Here's how to make it easy for them to work with you.

A *View of the Big Picture.* Remember that you're leading your newsletter team. Get everyone excited about the goals of the publication. Show volunteers previous issues of the publication and tell them about the positive changes or effects the newsletter has had. Sell volunteers on the success of your newsletter. People like to be involved with successes.

Short Commitments. Many people run from newsletter responsibility because it is a never-ending project. Issue after issue, year after year, this thing is going to be around. That's a huge commitment. Do not ask volunteers to make it.

Instead, break down jobs you need help with into onetime, easy-in/easy-out agreements. If someone enjoys working with you, they will volunteer again or agree to take on a longer-term task.

Precise Instructions. Conscientious writers, reporters and photographers fret over every aspect of their work. Provide them with precise instructions. This avoids rewrites or redos and preserves morale.

One of the most common problems occurs when contributors submit lengthy articles. The editor either must cut material or run an article that's going to turn away readers. If the editor changes the article, the volunteer is angry.

Protect volunteer morale. Provide length requirements (see *Counting Words for Articles* in Chapter 9, page 135). Provide forms that guide reporters to giving you exactly the information you need (see example, page 25). Give written instructions for photographers, artists, printers and desktop publishers. Respect the time of your volunteers.

Develop a style guide for writing headlines and articles, taking photographs and laying out the newsletter. (See Appendix 1.)

Scheduling. Another facet of respecting volunteer and vendor time is accurate scheduling of each step. When you have a schedule, you have a better feel for the amount and kind of help you're going to need, and you can recruit in advance instead of always at the last minute. You'll see the difference in every person involved with the newsletter—from contributors to paid vendors.

Develop a scheduling form for your newsletter. Give everyone involved a copy. Learn to schedule enough time for each step realistically and stick to the schedule.

REPORTER FORM

Newsletter: _____

Issue/Date: _____

Reporter Name: _____

Phone #: _____

Story Idea or Title: _____

_____

Who is involved/invited: _____
_____
_____

What is the event: _____
_____
_____

When did it (will it) happen: _____
_____
_____

Where: _____
_____
_____

Why did it (will it) happen: _____
_____
_____

How did it happen: _____
_____
_____

Other details: _____
_____
_____

Other people to contact: _____
_____
_____

Reporter forms such as this one make it easy to collect information that can be written into news style by the editor.

PROJECT SCHEDULE

Newsletter: _____

Issue/Date: _____

Task	Assigned To	Time Needed	Begin Date	Proof Date	Final Deadline
Define Content					
Approve Content					
Collect Information					
Write Articles					
Find/Create Graphics					
Edit Articles					
Approve Copy/Graphics					
Layout					
Proofread					
Produce Page Proofs					
Approve Page Proofs					
Print					
Run Mailing Labels					
Mail/Distribute					
Follow-up					
Other:					

Distribute your newsletter schedule to everyone involved in the newsletter. Reinforce the idea that missed deadlines affect all other steps of newsletter production.

EDITORIAL SCHEDULE

Newsletter: _____

Publication Year: _____

Issue Date	Feature:	Feature:	Feature:	Feature:	Notes:

Yearly editorial schedules organize the newsletter content into one cohesive effort. At a glance, you can see the future articles you'll need help with and the subjects you've already covered.

Training & Assisting. When you think of the people you respect, they are usually those who have pushed you to new heights—teachers, parents, managers, colleagues, friends—while also celebrating every success you've made along the way.

You can offer volunteers the benefit of your expertise—improving their newswriting and publishing skills. Someone may be a wonderful writer but one who writes such long articles that not many people are reading them. Such a writer may grumble the first time you insist on a 300-word maximum. But the increase in the number of people who read and comment on the shorter articles will ensure that the writer will thereafter support your policy wholeheartedly.

Recognition. Your recognition of your volunteer's efforts is an important first step. Recognition from readers is probably even more rewarding. When someone submits a reporter form for an article, list a byline "as reported by" as is done in many newspapers and magazines. Motivate and train volunteers to do good work, and people will comment on their efforts.

Give everyone on your newsletter team extra copies of each newsletter that they can give to their family and friends.

YOUR NETWORK OF REPORTERS & STRINGERS

Reporters and stringers scattered throughout the organization—sometimes throughout the country—are on the spot to turn up information and story ideas in their corners of the organization, where the editor cannot always be.

The challenges of working with these volunteers are real, but they are not insurmountable.

Bright, enthusiastic reporters turn stories in on time for each issue, then eagerly await the sight of their words in print. But they are not news writers. Their stories must be substantially rewritten before they see print. If their feelings are hurt by editing—and whose are not?—they may lose interest.

Clarify whether a volunteer is a reporter or a writer. If a reporter is interested in becoming a writer, invest the time to develop this volunteer's talents.

The editor must sit down with reporters and explain how a story is reworked into newswriting style. The editor who goes over a reporter's story, explaining from the first paragraph to the last the importance of journalistic techniques, has taken the first step to develop the reporter into a valuable writer. It will take several sessions, but with the right attitude on both parts, it will pay off.

A good editor, like a good parent, sets limits. Be tough about deadlines. Some reporters won't submit stories regularly or will always be late. Another problem reporter is the one who submits stories not only late, but also with most of the facts missing..."to be filled in later." When? It is already past deadline!

With computer transmission, this is not *so* serious a problem as it once was. In some situations over which the reporter has no control, valuable information (such as monthly government statistics) may be unavailable at the time of writing. In such cases, the new technology really shows its stuff: the reporter's story can be submitted on disk or via modem. (Electronic mail transmissions have the advantage of being non-computer specific; disks must be compatible with your own computer system.) Then, when the missing statistics come out, they can be sent by fax or e-mail, and inserted into the story. Still, all the technology in the world cannot substitute for a responsible reporter who gets the news in on time and gets it there right.

The editor can set an early deadline for articles from a less professional reporter, so there will be time to complete stories for publication. A better approach is to educate the reporter about the delays and additional costs that incomplete stories cause. Instill in reporters a sense of professional obligation. If this doesn't work, consider finding other volunteers.

It takes time and skill, but an editor can develop a good reliable team of reporters who regularly help cover the organization's news.

It is essential to continually encourage volunteer writers to be professional, to take their writing and their deadlines seriously.

Set realistic deadlines—not so close to publication that getting the copy into print on time involves numerous overnight mail charges or other expensive rushing around—yet not so far in advance that no one takes them seriously.

A strong editor has the courage—and the back-up copy—to throw out, or at least delay until a later issue, any story, photograph or illustration submitted after a deadline.

Reporters, photographers and artists within the organization often can provide the quality of work required for the newsletter. But sometimes they cannot.

HELP FROM OUTSIDE PROFESSIONALS

Sometimes a newsletter outgrows an editor with a volunteer staff. There is more, or more exacting, work than they can do well. Perhaps the editor identifies one area in which the newsletter is always weak. Photographs may not be sharp and in focus. The page design and desktop publishing may be lackluster. The offset printer may be making the end product of all the work that goes into the publication look shoddy and amateurish.

The editor faced with such problems has two choices: (1) to request additional professional staff or equipment, or (2) to contract for services with outside firms.

If the cost-effective choice is to hire staff or to buy equipment, the editor must consider how much responsibility and time this adds to an already long list of duties. It is nearly always a mistake to buy such expensive equipment as a Linotronic typesetting machine or a printing press unless they are to be used for many other projects besides the newsletter. In addition to the cost of the equipment itself, other expenses such as supplies, maintenance and paying an operator must be considered. A newsletter alone can seldom justify such expenditures.

Outside writing help can be bought—from individual freelancers, public relations firms or advertising agencies.

These are expensive. They are usually not practical for collecting routine information. But for feature articles, the outside professional writer who understands the organization and its goals can provide fresh, crisp copy for the newsletter.

Likewise, professional photographers and artists, properly directed by an editor, can vastly improve the graphic quality of a newsletter. They are professionals for a reason. That reason is ostensibly that they are good. They are also expensive. Shop around.

The editor seeking outside help needs to: (1) sit down with several professional photographers and writers and look at their portfolios, (2) assess their abilities in terms of the newsletter's purpose, (3) for writers, assure that articles can be submitted in electronic format to avoid re-keying, (4) get a clear understanding of their charges and (5) clear any contracts with the organization's bigwigs.

WHO'S IN CHARGE?

Once the editor has a good staff organized from talented help inside and outside the organization, the newsletter ought to be looking good and doing its job. One thing that can slow down the whole process, however, is confusion about who's in charge. You may think you are. Chances are you are not. You have the responsibility, all right. But you do not have free rein to call all of the shots about costs and contents of the newsletter. Not at first.

Almost invariably someone else has the final say about the budget and editorial content of the newsletter. And that someone may be one or—heaven help you—more bosses, or even a board.

Your relationship with whoever has final say about the newsletter is crucial to your—and the newsletter's—continuing success.

There are several typical problems in the editor/management relationship that may be resolved with immediate action and put into writing as part of your publication guidelines.

1. When more than one person has "final authority," the editor should sit down with them and agree on one person for this role. A second person may have preliminary authority—but only one can have final.

2. When policies exist about bidding for desktop publishing, printing, mailing, and dealing with other suppliers, the editor should discuss these with management and make sure there is a clear mutual understanding of what these policies are.

    Many government agencies and organizations that do business with the government, for instance, have specific quota requirements for minority or union contractors. They also have a set amount of money over which bids must be taken or board approval secured before expenditures can be made. Editors who do not understand and comply with such requirements can cause problems for themselves and their organizations.

    The editor and executive should agree on their understanding of these policies. And they should reach mutual understanding about how far within the confines of these policies the editor's authority properly extends.

3. When the person with final authority tries to control not only budget and editorial content, but also such details as format and other newsletter specifications, it is wise to discuss any changes in these areas in advance—especially if they are radical revisions. In general, it is a good idea to keep executives informed well in advance of all policy changes and decisions to which they must give approval.

4. When the final authority is too slow or too busy to sign off stories, get copy to him or her as early as possible. Keep checking back regularly—just short of badgering— to get approval in time for deadline.

    It is not unusual—although it is unfortunate—to have a final authority who insists on changing stories after the page layout is completed. The editor must convince such an executive that time is money. The time for changes is *before page layout begins*—after that any correction that changes the length of a line may also change the shape of a page and, with it, the cost of making the correction. It is disrespectful to the editor to keep asking for changes.

5. One regular contributor to many newsletters is the executive who has a monthly letter or column. Executives are a special case. But the editor must be as firm with executives as with other contributors. Teach even your biggest big bosses to meet deadlines, and help them with their writing as much as they are willing to let you. Establish maximum word counts for recurring columns and inform the boss's secretary. They'll appreciate your professionalism on behalf of the organization.

THE BOSS WHO CAN'T LET GO

Some executives can't seem to let go of any authority for the newsletter—as they probably can't let go of authority for anything else in the organization. The boss has management skills to develop. Meanwhile, editors can help. But first, the editor must understand the boss.

The executive wants to have final say not only about his or her monthly message to readers, but about every aspect of the newsletter from budgeting and editorial content to sentence construction.

You can understand this. The executive is the person with the high public profile. The external newsletter represents the organization to the public. Employees and members perceive their organization primarily through the insiders' newsletter. These newsletters are important. The executive wants to make sure they're doing the job envisioned for them.

For this reason, the number of editors who are able to walk into a job and instantly have complete say about what goes into "their" newsletters is very small.

It isn't easy, but you can wrest this overweening concern from the boss and return it to its proper sphere—yours. You not only can do it, you must do it. It is extremely important to reach the point at which the executive has the confidence in your judgment and ability to stop interfering with your work.

Work to establish a healthy rapport with executives. Exude knowledgeable professionalism, control and confidence. Learn how they think and what they want—and act on it.

Only when executives feel an editor's intensely alert loyalty to the organization (which is to say their own philosophies) will they loosen the strings on the editorial content and budget.

It is a great day in the lives of the executive and editor alike when this happens, for then they are free to go about their respective duties.

Remember, such executives don't think they want you to have responsibility for their newsletter. But they do. And the editor who wrests it away will be paid for this competence many times over.

One last note: Don't run the boss's column on the front page with a standing head (Message from the Chair, etc.) and a mug shot. Even if your bigwig doesn't know better, you should.

WHAT EQUIPMENT IS AVAILABLE?

As you assess the eager talent that may be available for sprucing up the newsletter operation, look around at the existing equipment to see what might contribute to the newsletter's overall quality.

Is there a dependable computer available, with the power, RAM, and disk space to run a good desktop publishing software program? Do you have access to a scanner for reproducing photographs on the computer? Does the system contain a selection of typefaces acceptable for good, strong headlines and legible body copy?

The ideal situation, of course, is to have such a desktop publishing system for your own—and many editors do. But it is not an ideal world. The '80s are long gone, and many budgets have been stretched to the breaking point. So some time-sharing may be in your future.

If the computer is in someone else's bailiwick, can you have access to it on a dependable basis? Will you know how to run it? If someone else must teach you or run it for you, can the joys of computer education and/or newsletter production be added to his or her present schedule without unfair burden?

IN-HOUSE VS. OUTSIDE PAGE LAYOUT

If you consider outside page layout and printing, the main consideration is cost. Get some estimates and bids.

A desktop publishing service estimates that typesetting a four-page newsletter will cost between $300 and $400. A printer estimates that printing 2,000 newsletters will cost $500 plus $10 for each halftone (photograph).

"Too much," you say. "We'll continue doing it the way we've been doing it." You may want to consider hidden cost factors.

1. If your computer operator is paid $8 to $10 an hour, and if it takes 10 to 20 hours to lay out each newsletter, getting the margins just so, fooling with the page layout, making corrections, tying up the computer system, changing whole pages when some last-minute copy change is made, then typesetting your newsletter in-house costs between $80 and $200.

2. Using a copier may cost from two to five cents a page, plus an additional penny or two a sheet for the paper. Say a four-page newsletter is two sheets printed on both sides, and the cost per copy is four cents. The cost of copying each newsletter will be 16 cents, or $320 for 2,000 newsletters, in addition to the staff time of operating the copier and the drawback of tying up the equipment.

Another consideration is that each printed page requires a master plate, and once that plate is prepared, the printer can run off innumerable copies. The more copies printed, the lower the cost per copy, since the fixed price of the plate is distributed over the total press run. The bigger the circulation, the greater the cost advantage of printing.

Although there may be cost advantages to doing all of your own production work, make sure the quality of your in-house layout is up to professional standards and that the time the project takes from other (possibly more profit-generating) tasks is worth the savings.

This is not to say that typesetting and offset printing are the only way to go. Even a modest newsletter, written, edited and typed entirely by the editor and reproduced on the office copying machine, may be excellent for its purpose and circulation. It may look good and speak well to the readers it serves. (See *The Word Processed Newsletter* in Chapter 9, page 124.)

Each organization has its unique combination of talent and equipment with varying capabilities. Perhaps there is little talent to tap, but if you need reporters badly, it may be worth your time to train some. This will be especially challenging if you have departments or chapters or affiliates from Maine to Mexico. Think of the bright side. If you can't train people long-distance, you've just added travel to your job description.

Chapter 4

Target
the News

*Editors strive to strike a balance
among loyalty to the organization, credibility
to the audience and personal integrity.*

Is There News in a Newsletter?

In the big, worldly sense, there's probably not much news in a newsletter—not like there is, say, in *The New York Times*. *The Times* reflects the great world—it is, in fact, a "paper of record," which means it tries to record all the significant events in the world each day. A big job. A great paper.

Newsletters don't have such a big job, and yet many organizations are practically a world unto themselves. People working in a large hospital, insurance company—any large institution or business—reflect the organization's values and philosophy. Unconsciously, perhaps, they think in company terms, speak company jargon. They are in many ways a true community. Association members, donors and volunteers, likewise, although often distant physically, are philosophically or socially a community. Customers comprise a community of people interested in the same products and services.

What's news in your community? Everything is "news" to someone. The trick is to recognize what is news to your readers.

Inside News Sources

Some reliable sources of legitimate news inside almost any organization are listed below. Editors may gather such news themselves; in a very large association, non-profit organization or company, on-site reporters and offsite stringers help gather it as noted above.

Meetings. Significant meetings involving progress or policy, such as regular monthly board meetings, reveal some information that will be of interest to newsletter readers. Professional association meetings and conventions attended by one or more staff members provide newsworthy reports. Ideally the editor covers all important meetings in person, to catch the spirit of the occasion (if any) and such details and lively dialogue as are not captured in official minutes.

When minutes or secondhand accounts of meetings are all the editor has to work with, an interview with one or more of the participants should add some life and color to a meeting story.

Reports, Research Findings & White Papers. Different departments or chapters issue reports from time to time. These reports at first glance may seem obscure, even opaque—perhaps a bit boring. But reports can be searched for items of actual significance to the people in the organization. An interview with the person who prepared the new budget may net explanations and quotes that will clarify the meaning of those rows of statistics in the lives of people.

Management & Personnel Announcements. Announcements of a major expansion or restructuring, additional products or expanded services are, of course, cause for front page coverage, as are the occasions of major grants or contracts involving the organization.

Memos about new policies, reports about revised programs or new equipment should be examined for possible stories—or short story items at the least.

Good reporters read between the lines of the seemingly insignificant announcement and interview management for details and quotes to get a story that will interest readers.

For employee newsletters, the human resources department is a prime source for stories of new employees, promotions, transfers, retirements; it also supplies items about changes in work and vacation schedules, improvements in insurance and other benefits.

Speeches. Top officers frequently give speeches at national meetings or to local groups such as the Kiwanis Club. Often the newsletter editor helps write the speech. Do not overlook speeches as a good source of news stories, even if you did write them!

External Press Releases. Often, newsletters are underutilized as a continuation of an organization's public relations effort. Scan your own press releases. Employees and clients need to know about all new products and services. Add more life and interest for your audience by interviewing and adding the insights you find.

OUTSIDE NEWS SOURCES

As no man is an island, no organization is an island. The world of the newsletter may be small, but it is not closed. It is affected by laws. It is affected by attitudes and trends.

News from the Lawmakers. State, local and federal government bodies regulate and/or support many industries and agencies. They are constantly brewing new regulations and passing new laws that affect the nation's businesses, professional organizations and charities. They can make or break programs overnight. The upshot of complicated regulations can be garnered from such publications as the daily *Federal Register* and communicated to an interested audience in plain English. This is not easy. But the conscientious editor will learn to interpret, or find someone on the staff who knows how to interpret, significant rules and regulations affecting his organization.

For government agencies and federally funded programs, this information is not only of interest, it is vital.

News from Other Publications. Readers want and need to know about related industries and professional organizations throughout the country. Physical therapists are interested in developments and news about the health care industry at large. Contractors want to know about improvements in concrete-mixing techniques and about interest rates on home loans. Editors scan trade publications for new developments, ideas and information.

Stories may be written from these sources, quoting the source and emphasizing how the local organization is affected by the news. Quoting a knowledgeable source within the local organization is always a good practice to bring sharp focus to such a story.

News of National & International Import. Reporting such news is not ordinarily the task of the organizational newsletter. But if oil prices rising in Saudi Arabia or gold prices falling in London directly affect your organization in some identifiable way, the newsletter properly reports on that effect.

Such a report is not written off the top of the editor's head. Interpretation by the president or the financial officer or the board chairman—a responsible, authoritative spokesperson—is proper. The story can be an interview, or a composite of opinions from various sources. An editor who is particularly well versed in the subject may want to add his or her own analysis.

SERIES & FEATURES

Any number of series can be created to run issue after issue. These aren't strictly news. But they're high interest, high readership items in any publication from *The New Yorker* to the organizational newsletter. It is always a good idea to include one or more feature series to add variety to a publication.

A series needn't last forever. Set up and run a four-, six-, or twelve-part series—whatever you have—identifying it as such with each issue. Readers gain a certain satisfaction from series. They like knowing something is going to be there issue after issue, something with a predictable and comfortable familiarity.

Highlight Series. Highlights of people—customers, employees-of-the-month, members, or volunteers—are gratifying to their subjects and interesting to other readers. Highlights can also be of products and services. Any organization with a good supply of interesting programs or products could run highlight series on them as a regular column.

Profiles of Executives. Profiles of executive officers and board members acquaint employees with the individuals who set policy. They communicate something of why the organization is the way it is and where it is headed. Knowledge of what important people think creates a sense of identification, harmony and well-being among workers or members.

At the same time, carefully balance the editorial space devoted to executives with that dedicated to customers or employees. The number, size and placement of executive articles can unintentionally signal a bias to readers, telling them you see only from the organization's or management's point of view.

Profiles of important individuals outside the immediate organization—a powerful leader or expert in the same field, a politician committed to legislative changes that affect the industry, an influential individual who has frequent dealings with the organization—can be valuable aids to employee understanding of how the company fits into the larger picture. Such stories flatter the individuals featured and build goodwill with them for the organization.

History. Reprints from old newsletters and annual reports and interviews with old-timers, retiring employees or founders can go into a series on the history of the organization.

One of the most popular columns in a large community hospital newsletter in San Francisco is a history column written by a long-time staff physician, a descendant of some of the founders, who very much enjoys writing it.

History columns dramatize what it was like during crucial periods such as the great depression or the energy crisis. They promote a sense of continuity and tradition in younger people, and they build pride in the organization. Besides, they are fun to do.

Inquiring Photographer. The inquiring photographer or "speak up" column is created by asking a question of four or five people and running their answers to it along with their photographs. A typical question for an employee newsletter might be: "What is your opinion of the flex time experiment now being tried?" Or for a customer newsletter: "How has the XYZ widget helped your business?"

The answers are kept short, usually only one to three short paragraphs. Strive for lively questions, but clear them with key people first. Seek answers that show more than one side of an issue. A round-up article enhances a newsletter's feeling of community.

Editorials & Opinion Columns. This is the place for organizational propaganda. Contributed editorials and guest columns are clearly labeled as being from management or board members, executives or experts. Reprints of editorials from other publications are good sources, too, if they are relevant to your organization. The source should be asked for permission and given credit.

Here again, strive for lively subjects. Editorials appearing in each issue, such as a letter from the president, need headlines that reflect the article's content. Avoid "Letter from the President" using instead "Employees Choose Flex Time." (See *15 Ways to Write Good Headlines* in Chapter 7, page 96.)

Book Reviews. Reviews of books pertinent to an organization's activity are interesting to readers. If your circulation is big enough, most publishers will supply books, and there are usually staff or members willing to review a book for the privilege of keeping it. But if you can afford it, pay a good reviewer something—even if it is only $25 or $50—in appreciation of the fact that a good review involves many hours of work. (Most publishers will send a press release or sample book review along with the book. Add your own opinions and customize the review for your audience.)

Letters to the Editor. These columns are sometimes hard to get going, but they are valuable because they involve readers and make the newsletter in part really the readers'. Discreet editing helps keep the letters short.

Some letter columns evolve into advocacy forums where complaints, suggestions and ideas are aired between employees or members and management, but this role is limited to the insiders' newsletters only.

Comics, Cartoons, Puzzles. Regular features that give readers a laugh are always popular. The problem is finding a good, relevant source. Staff volunteer efforts may be relevant but unprofessional. Professional humorists may be masterful but irrelevant. A specific cartoon by a major cartoonist may sometimes be reprinted with permission. Write for it. Syndicates sell humor features and puzzles and the like on a subscription basis. Check *Writer's Market* for listings under Syndicates and write for samples and prices.

Promotions. Continuing update stories about the United Fund Drive, the blood bank or other civic efforts contribute to the success of those efforts and help the organization's image in the community.

If plant safety is an issue, run a regular item of "days without an accident" figures along with safety advice.

Firms in business to sell products are full of competitive salespeople who want to know how they measure up. Who's producing the most? Who's delivering the service that customers comment favorably on? How do they do it? How does the company compare with others selling similar products? What do *they* know that *we* don't know?

Pass around good ideas and techniques that the sales force uses. Let them contribute material for this column. Nothing succeeds like—or reads like—success!

Feature Stories. Many of the ideas discussed here might properly be called features or special features and most could be developed as feature stories. Feature story is difficult to define because it means so many things. Generally, it connotes a story that is interesting for reasons other than its value as hard news. The feature story is discussed in more detail in Chapter 6.

THE MULTIPLE AUDIENCE DILEMMA

Newsletter editors often face the dilemma of addressing more than one special-interest audience at a time. The common interest of employees and outside readers may end with major news of the organization's progress. Then what?

If most of the readers of a newsletter are clients and other people outside the organization, news of the annual picnic, births and weddings, or minor staff changes are of little interest to the major readership and should be played down. But if most of the readers are employees, then such stories are appropriate, and are, in fact, what the readers want.

Serving an organization's employees is extremely important. They must not be ignored. Studies show that most employees judge their working places by their perception of top management, a perception gained primarily through the organizational newsletter.

Editors with large numbers of employee readers and outside readers often resolve this dilemma by publishing two newsletters—one for each audience.

In most cases, employees receive both publications, outside readers only the external publication. One Chicago agency alternates months, publishing an employee newsletter one month, an external newsletter the next. Other organizations print special inserts that go into employee copies of the external publication, but not into the other copies.

A common practice in many places is to publish a simple, photocopied newsletter for employees each week or month, and a more elaborate, offset-printed monthly newsletter for a large outside audience.

Some large insurance companies and businesses put out a daily employee bulletin—one sheet, with or without photographs, depending on the copying method.

WHAT'S NEWS IN EMPLOYEE PUBLICATIONS?

If a publication is heavily employee oriented, or strictly for employees, these kinds of news items (in addition to those mentioned previously) are probably appropriate, and will have high readership:

1. Sports scores of company teams
2. Weather forecasts (in a daily)
3. Features on outstanding or unusual employee hobbies, achievements, vacations
4. Information about staff changes, benefit changes, etc.
5. Health, nutrition, self-improvement columns.

In a strictly employee or alumni publication, vital statistics—i.e., births, deaths and marriages—are vitally interesting to readers.

Because people like to read about themselves and those they work with, there is a nearly unlimited source of feature story material at hand for the enterprising editor of an employee publication.

A company canoe trip or picnic can be covered as a feature story—complete with lively dialogue and colorful description of the surroundings. Or a story can be written with suspense and drama about the security officer who captured drug thieves in the hospital dispensary.

Stories about employees' and their families' outstanding or unusual achievements and hobbies, vacations, and other leisure activities are well read in employee circles: Mike Jonas wins a citywide kite flying contest; Nelda Green's daughter, Tracy, wins a forestry scholarship to the state university; Joe Adamson catches the biggest channel cat anyone's seen in Rockaway County since '58; Marty Roberts has a fascinating collection of, would you believe, pygmy artifacts.

Features like these make the people—and the work along with them—seem less routine. They say, "We are interesting individuals in our own right—with lives and achievements worth noting."

FINDING THE RIGHT TONE

Many newsletters grow with the organization. As the organization gets too big or employees too scattered to make communication by word of mouth, bulletin boards and memos practical, a newsletter is started. It often becomes the principal means of communication between an organization's management and its employees.

Good communication leads to other results. For instance, employee newsletters have been shown to increase productivity by boosting morale and by helping employees understand how their jobs fit into the overall company effort. Since it is so important, the employee newsletter should be approached intelligently and thoughtfully. At the heart of the effective employee-oriented newsletter is the right editorial tone.

If the newsletter assumes the stance of Pronouncement from on High, as the Official Voice of Management, its communications effectiveness is badly damaged. No one wants to be talked down to or preached to, or told what to do.

On the other hand, if the newsletter relies solely on gossipy chit-chat, it doesn't provide real, substantive communication. Experienced editors of employee newsletters keep plenty of solid information coming at readers, and plenty of stories about the readers themselves.

Positive messages from management are presented matter-of-factly. It is unprofessional to "gush" in print. Negative messages from management are extremely low key in presentation—implied or stated subtly. An editor should never forget that a vital function of an employee newsletter is to improve employee morale.

A long-term series of studies has shown that almost *any* change intended to improve the work environment increases productivity. The reason: people work better if they think that the people they work for are concerned about them. If management makes changes, employees feel their welfare is important. So if a newsletter can help effect needed changes in response to suggestions by employees, it contributes substantially to improving morale, and hence to efficiency and better production within the organization. Even if it doesn't effect the changes, it publicizes them, which is equally important.

A good job provides more than money. Some important job-satisfaction indicators are how important employees perceive their jobs to be, and how much individual recognition is given for the work they do. Stories explaining how a person's job is related to the overall success of the organization—and stories reporting outstanding work by employees or awards given for such work—do much to help employee morale.

Equally important are stories pointing out company achievements or good deeds (civic contributions, foundation grants, etc.), stories that every employee can be proud of, and stories that demon-strate that employees are being fairly rewarded for their efforts.

A newsletter that accomplishes such goals as increasing produc-tivity and improving morale and attitude in the working place is doing its job and doing it well.

THE EXTERNAL NEWSLETTER

If you edit both the employee and marketing newsletters, you must change hats when you sit down to write the customer publication. Customers care more about what you offer than who you are. They need product information, news of changing services, information on how to better use your products, and summaries of what's hap-pening in your industry and how your company fits in.

The tone of the customer newsletter must be written from the customer's point of view. A good way to assure this is to phrase news in terms of "you" instead of "we."

For example, if your company introduces a new invoicing sys-tem, your first response will be to think of it from your point of view. You would write, "We at XYZ Corporation are introducing a new invoicing system that will save us time each month and improve account collections." Rethink your approach from the customer's perspective. Write "As a direct response to customer feedback, your monthly invoices are being updated. The new format is easier to read and understand. You'll also receive a return envelope."

THE EDITOR AS ADVOCATE

The professional newsletter editor is a hired gun, an advocate. You work for an organization; that organization pays you to represent it to the public. Your first duty is to the organization and its goals. (The volunteer editor is subject to the same expectations.)

So you pay attention to what the executive officers conceive to be in the best interest of the company, and work that vein of news.

This is not to say that you are a slave to the whims of anyone higher up the organizational ladder than you. Some people get nervous, especially under pressure. Then they get bad ideas. No one gains personal respect—or respect for a publication or an organization—by complying with demands to print outrageous, misleading or false information.

When a publication loses its credibility, it loses everything. So, editors strive to strike a balance among loyalty to the organization, credibility to the audience and personal integrity.

You can be firm, faithful to the facts and fair—and still find a lot of room for advocacy within the confines of honest reporting. It all depends on what you choose to emphasize. You emphasize what makes the organization look good.

Even major newspapers, busily criticizing and exposing ills in the community, seldom criticize themselves. Reporters on major dailies are sometimes asked to cover an insignificant or undesirable story because the publisher wants to promote some pet project. Worse, they are sometimes asked to ignore or slant stories—much more serious offenses for a publication purporting to serve the public than for a newsletter expected by its nature to advocate a particular point of view.

The great majority of newspapers, organizations and companies act in good faith. They try to do the right thing and do it well. They make mistakes, too. But an editor can help an organization grow stronger and better—in its own and in the public eye—by emphasizing what it does right.

For example, here's a story with great reader appeal: The consultants who just spent three years around the city planning office, drinking coffee, talking to secretaries, and spending $300,000 of taxpayers' money, produced an equivocal report—it looks as if the result is, well, *nothing*.

Do you, the editor of the city hall newsletter, write the story and run it?

No.

Running that story would hurt your organization. So you ignore it, or better still, try to find *some* positive result to report, perhaps how the study is *expected* to save the taxpayers $4 million. If the local press gets the story and writes an expose, you are even more obliged to produce a story showing any value that can be found in the study.

The newsletter, like the optimist, accentuates the positive and eliminates the negative. There are times, however, when the negative shouldn't be ignored.

If problems, complaints or rumors within an organization demand attention, the newsletter may be the place to resolve or clarify them. You can interview people about a problem and get different ideas of what should be done. Focusing attention on real rather than imagined issues may well work them out. Printing the truth behind a rumor often eliminates the rumor.

The newsletter editor who knows when to use news and when to ignore it, the firmly loyal and credible professional editor, is a valuable member of the organizational team.

Chapter 5

Gather the News

Experienced reporters know that it is a good idea to get as much information as possible firsthand.

MAINTAINING JOURNALISTIC OBJECTIVITY

The newsletter editor, although an advocate, retains some professional journalistic objectivity without undue agonizing. Hard factual news is handled one way, interpretative features another. Editorials are identified clearly as opinion material. So far so good.

Yet the editor's basic function is to exercise subjective judgment—which, while it is educated opinion, is still opinion. The editor decides which stories to run and which to drop. Judgment. The editor decides which words, sentences and paragraphs stay in stories and which go. Judgment. The editor knows that the journalistic ideal of complete objectivity is just that—an ideal.

The editor who is also a news writer knows that *the best chance to approximate this much touted impartiality is in thorough news gathering, getting all sides—or as many sides as possible—of the story.* The honorable journalistic ideal of objectivity lives on in stories that are conscientiously researched and accurately reported.

This means gathering as much information for a story as time allows, through phone and leg work: interviewing principals, interviewing outsiders or the opposition, and searching through existing files and stories. It also means guarding the publication's credibility and legal liability.

PRIME NEWS SOURCES

News sources are myriad, but fall roughly into three categories:
1. Firsthand observation and interviews with principals.
2. What other people say.
3. Printed and other media stories, contemporary or historical.

Experienced reporters know that it is a good idea to get as much information as possible firsthand, by observation and interview of principal persons and events. They try to be where the action is, which, in the newsletter world, may mean something as seemingly unexciting as a committee meeting, speech, conference or groundbreaking ceremony.

But being there offers the opportunity to talk with participants, including those who deliver important reports or speeches. If something highly technical is involved, this is a chance to clarify the point so readers will understand what has actually happened. It is also a chance to enliven a story with quotes.

The alternative to being there, as the ads keep telling us, is using the telephone. Technically, whenever you pick up the phone to ask someone a question about a story, you are conducting an interview. The telephone is valuable as a quick way to check facts and the spellings of names and to obtain additional information to round out a story. Of course, you can get an entire story via the telephone, and this is sometimes necessary if you are pressed for time or if the interviewee is far away. Whenever possible, however, it is preferable to interview news sources in person.

INTERVIEWING LIKE A PRO

The interview, whether a quick one-question abbreviated one or a full-blown two-hour one, is a fact of life for writers and editors. A casual conversation with the boss at the water cooler about the implications of a memo on office dress code is an interview. A chance meeting with a fellow club member at the grocery can turn into an interview. A few questions asked to a customer while taking an order may be an interview. It is good manners and good politics to let people know they're being interviewed in such chance encounters.

Any reluctance to interview news sources hampers the abilities of an otherwise good reporter. Yet, often writers don't want to do interviews. They're unsure of their ability to conduct a good one. Or they are afraid the person to be interviewed is "too busy" and will resent giving them time.

There is only one way to overcome this reluctance. Master interviews by doing a lot of them. Interview people whenever possible. The more interviews, the more skillful the interviewer becomes.

And most people, no matter how busy or important they are, are flattered, secretly at least, that they are considered interesting enough to be interviewed. For a story about an important person, the interview is essential. There is no other way, really, to get the story. At least, there is no better way.

Some seasoned experts and celebrities will try to get the jump on you by attempting to conduct an interview by mail. They will ask for written questions and send back their written answers. The problem with this is simply that the questions are lifeless, and the answers will be lifeless. It is not a real interview. The result is an unsatisfying mixture of the too formal and the suspiciously phony. There is no satisfactory substitute for being there.

PREPARING QUESTIONS FOR THE INTERVIEW

To be a successful interviewer, psych up for an interview. First, fix clearly in mind why this person is a good source—what he or she knows that the readers will want to know. What questions should you ask? The expert who can shed light on a subject that seems opaque to the average reader's mind may answer such a question as "What does 'creative financing' mean, exactly?"

The newly appointed president interests readers generally. They want to know all about him. Ask. "What are your strengths? Your weaknesses? What are your plans for the future of the organization?"

A highly paid consultant has just been hired. Rumors buzz. Readers want to know why she's worth her fee. "What previous projects have you done? What were the results?" Ask questions outright, even if you don't expect a straight answer. An elusive answer or no answer is still an answer—more than you get if you never ask. And such answers often reveal a lot.

DOING YOUR HOMEWORK

If you are hazy about what to ask the person to be interviewed, some homework is in order. Some basic background facts need to be ascertained. Who is this person, exactly? This is where other people and earlier news stories can help.

Ask other people who know about the interviewee; dig up previous stories from other publications. If the person is clearly representing one side of an issue, gather information presenting the other side.

The more sources and sides of an issue explored, the better the chance of getting information that will round out a good story.

Perhaps the subject of the story has come up before. Consult clips of previous stories.

Finding out all you can before an interview—through other people and sources—accomplishes two things. It enables you to better plan the range of questions to ask, and it eliminates the need for asking a lot of what the interviewee will justly perceive as dumb questions at the opening of the interview.

Nothing irritates an important person more than being asked things he prefers to believe everyone already knows about his stellar career. You can't open an interview with Al Gore by fixing on him with a pleasantly interested smile and asking what he does for a living.

CONDUCTING THE INTERVIEW

Set a specific time for the interview. Allow time—probably at least an hour—to ask enough questions to adequately cover the subject, to over-cover it, really, because it is always better to have too much information than not enough.

Find out all you can before the interview. Then write down a list of questions. Many times, the person being interviewed will drift off the topic and into new, perhaps more interesting territory. That's all right. But there will be a lull, and that's when you can get back on track by consulting your list of questions.

Start out in a conversational way, without pad and pencil. The time to start taking notes is after you both are comfortable and the interview has more or less formally begun.

Good interviewers write fast, usually using a personal shorthand system. But beginners, and some experienced practitioners, may find a subject reeling off quote after quotable quote. If you just can't keep up, ask the subject to wait until you catch up. The subject is just as eager as you are to have quotes appear in print accurate and complete.

Another way around this problem is to use a tape recorder.

This is a simple solution, but like most simple solutions, it has drawbacks. One, the subject may not like to be taped. Two, it takes skill and luck to accurately record everything in a conversation, including gestures and throwaway phrases. And three, there's Murphy's law: anything that can go wrong will go wrong. There's always a good chance the recorder will malfunction and leave you high and dry and very embarrassed to ask for another interview.

Even if the recorder functions properly and every sigh and chortle is captured, a taped interview can be time-consuming and inefficient. You must go back to the office, replay the tape, and then begin the painful process of extracting the important parts of the interview. Nothing is more frustrating than running a tape back and forth seeking that "great quote" you know is on there somewhere. By taping, you are merely *delaying the actual process of writing.*

Taking notes *and* running a tape may be the best policy. Set your tape recorder's counter to "0" at the beginning of the interview (or simply note the start time on your watch). When your subject says something you know you want to quote, discreetly note the number on the recorder (or the time) along with a key word or two in your written notes. The writing is started, the high points are on paper, and the tape will serve as a back-up only, not as the principal source.

Transcribe notes into your word processor as soon after the interview as possible. Rapidly scribbled words sometimes can't be recalled if too much time elapses between the writing and the typing of them. A single word on a note pad may stand for an entire sentence. Fill in the missing parts quickly or you will forget them. If you have time, go ahead and quickly write a rough draft of the article. Then, let it sit until you have time to finish the piece.

KEEPING GOOD FILES

Organized editors keep good files. Old newsletters, memos, reports and clippings are kept in usable order. Good files are indispensable. They save time. They fill out stories that would otherwise be too sketchy or too obviously one-sided. They promote accuracy.

Functional filing systems employ simple, logical categories: names, subject matter, project or department titles, filed A to Z. Order and logic mean easy retrieval of information by anyone who needs to use the files. If they are skimpy or haphazard, or if they look like overstuffed chairs, they won't be used. Much time and energy is necessary to organize a workable filing system. But the time will be well spent, and the effort will pay for itself many times over.

A physical filing system includes photographs of principal members of the organization who are often the subjects of newsletter stories. It includes photographs shot for use in previous publications, whether they were used or not.

Many editors keep files electronically. Stories that weren't used, future ideas for articles, rough notes from interviews and texts of memos or press releases are stored on disk, ready for a future issue. Electronic files may also include scanned photographs and news clips or records of what is stored in your physical files.

PROTECTING CREDIBILITY

A publication's credibility depends on accuracy, fairness and consistency. Each issue, each story, affects credibility. Note significant errors in one issue and print corrections in the next. Establish a reputation as a conscientious editor.

Be alert to the special credibility problem of newsletters: stories that seem to issue from on high, that carry no attribution, even for very opinionated material. "Who," the reader will ask, "says so?" The reader has a right to know not only the facts and opinions themselves, but also who is stating them.

```
▤▯▭▬▬▬ Newsletter Folder ▬▬▬▱▭▤
 9 items          147.9 MB in disk      12.9 MB availabl
┌─────────────────────────────────────────────┬───┐
│  📁 1995 Editorial Schedule                   │ ⬆ │
│                                               │   │
│  📁 Artwork for Each Issue                    │   │
│  📁 Employee Photos                           │   │
│  📁 Filler Items                              │   │
│  📁 Idea File                                 │   │
│  📁 News Clippings                            │   │
│  📁 Press Releases                            │   │
│  📁 Product Photos                            │   │
│  📁 Submitted Articles                        │   │
│                                               │   │
│                                               │ ⬇ │
├───────────────────────────────────────┬───┬───┤
│ ⬅                                       │ ➡ │ 🗗 │
└─────────────────────────────────────────┴───┴───┘
```

Your filing system may exist solely on your computer's hard drive. Set up ideas and articles in files just as you would in a regular filing cabinet.

Some editors believe that to avoid controversy and ignore adverse opinion is to protect the organization. But such a policy may, in fact, hurt credibility. Often, a controversy met head on, in print, with fair representation of all sides, can be honorably resolved. Ignoring criticism won't make it go away. Take the opportunity to present your side of the issue and to put it in the best possible light. Negative gossip and criticism spread quite naturally all by themselves. Use the newsletter to present the positive side. Demonstrate that there is nothing to hide, that your group is doing what it sincerely believes is right.

WATCHING FOR LEGAL PROBLEMS

The First Amendment to the U.S. Constitution guarantees freedom of speech and press. But this is a *qualified* freedom, preceded by obligations. Freedom of speech is limited by laws pertaining to libel, privacy and copyright.

Libel. Newsletter editors seldom venture into the dangerous journalistic waters of reporting trials, criminal activities or politics. Still, many libel suits spring from innocent mistakes such as mistaken identification or misplaced photographs, and you need at least a working knowledge of what these laws are about, because they can affect you just as they affect editors of national periodicals.

A libel has four elements:

1. *It must include a defamatory statement.* That's a statement that "holds a person up to public ridicule, contempt or hatred, causes him to be shunned or avoided, hurts his reputation, damages his credit, or injures him in his business or profession."

2. *The statement must be published.* Publication can be by words, pictures or other means, and courts have held that a statement is published if only one person other than the writer and victim sees it.

3. *The victim must be identified.* Even if his or her name doesn't appear in print, it is enough if the reader can infer who is meant.

4. *There must be injury.* But the law holds certain statements automatically injurious: those imputing a crime, low moral character, a loathsome disease or insanity.

The law of libel is different in each of the 50 states, but these are the essential elements in all of them.

In all states, anyone connected with a libel may be sued, but as a practical matter, the victim usually sues whoever has the money—in the present case, your organization.

Victims who win libel suits may collect general damages (whatever a judge or jury considers reasonable), special damages (actual monetary loss) and punitive damages (if they can show malice).

There are three basic defenses for the publishers:

1. Proving the truth of the statement and the *absence of malice*.
2. Proving that there was a qualified privilege to print the information (e.g., from an official court record).
3. Proving that there was a right of *fair comment*, applicable in criticizing any work of art (e.g., a play or a book) that has been offered for public approval.

A published retraction of a statement or photo that attracts the accusation of libel is not a defense but will show good intent and help reduce damages.

Strive for truth and accuracy in reporting. If you venture into controversial areas, say a lawsuit in which the organization is involved, exercise special care. Consult the company lawyer and clear what you write *before* it is published.

Privacy. The right of privacy is a person's right to be left alone. This law is vague and varies from state to state. But several points are clear and are pertinent to the newsletter editor.

1. Anything newsworthy that happens in public can be reported.
2. A public figure loses some claim to privacy.
3. The right to privacy ends when a person consents to publication. Consent is implied if he or she agrees to an interview.
4. A person's name or photograph can't be used for monetary gain without his or her consent. Get a release.
5. Truth is not a defense.

Copyright. The 1978 copyright law allows a person to copyright original works of literature, art, music, etc., for his or her lifetime plus 50 years.

Facts or news cannot be copyrighted, but the actual wording of an account of those facts can be. Writers drawing from copyrighted material may paraphrase it, and the convention is to give credit to the copyright holder. If you want to reprint an article, photograph, cartoon or illustration, get written permission (see form on next page).

Work done for the federal government cannot be copyrighted. This law permits free use of the oceans of material prepared by government agencies. The U.S. Government Printing Office is the largest publisher in the United Sates.

If an employee creates a "work for hire," e.g., for an employer, the employer is considered the author and may obtain a copyright on the work unless there has been an expressly written agreement between the two specifying otherwise.

Shield Laws. Most states have shield laws, laws protecting reporters from naming the source of information; but these laws limit this protection to employees of the news media and exclude newsletter writers and freelancers.

Gathering interesting content for your newsletter is an important first step in writing interesting articles. With your files full and notes in hand, it is time to whip your articles into shape using professional news writing techniques.

COPYRIGHT ASSIGNMENT

Name of publication: _____

Please complete and return promptly to:

> *your name & address here*

Name: _____

Address: _____

I am licensing to _____ :

❏ One-Time Use: I hereby grant the rights for one-time use (the copying, distributing, displaying, performing, and derivating) of the work(s) in the above-listed publication for:
_____

❏ First-Time Use: I hereby grant the rights for one-time use (the copying, distributing, displaying, performing, and derivating) of the work(s) in the above-listed publication for:
_____

❏ Exclusive License: I hereby grant the exclusive right(s) to use the work(s) for:
_____

❏ Non-Exclusive: I hereby grant non-exclusive license to copy, distribute, display publicly, perform publicly, and derivate the work(s) for: _____

I warrant that the material submitted is an original work of authorship authored and owned solely by myself and does not violate any other person or entity's copyright, trademark, rights of publicity, right of privacy, and/or any other such right.

I agree that any submitted material is subject to editing and that publication cannot be guaranteed. I acknowledge the ownership of copyright rights in any edited version belongs to the publisher as original creations of derivative works. If I sell the submitted material for use in any other magazine or other medium, I acknowledge that I do not have the right to use the edited version. Further, I am licensing nonexclusive rights for the use of the produced work(s), at no additional compensation, in any of the publisher's promotional material.

Title of work(s):_____ Payment: _____

Executed this _____ day of _____, 19____

_____   _____
Author/Artist Signature   Publication Signature

Set up a standardized form for requesting reprint permission. Some authors charge a reprint fee while others will grant permission in return for the publicity your newsletter gives.

WORKS FOR HIRE AGREEMENT

your name & address here

Artist/Writer: _____

Address: _____

_____

Phone #: _____

Publication Name: _____

I hereby assign to the company listed above ("the Company") and/or its clients any and all copyright and/or other intellectual property rights I may have in the material listed below and submitted to the Company.

To the extent permitted by copyright laws, the work submitted is a work for hire. In the event that this work is not a work for hire, any and all copyright rights are assigned to the Company.

I warrant that the work(s) assigned are unpublished, original works of authorship authored and owned solely by myself and does not violate any other person or entity's copyright, trademark, rights of publicity, right of privacy, and/or any other such right.

Title of Work(s): _____

Payment:_____

Date:_____

Artist's/Writer's signature:

_____

When you subcontract work, the writers and artists own the copyright to the work they create for you. You're essentially buying a one-time usage unless they agree to sign a "works for hire" agreement as shown here.

Chapter 6

Professional Writing & Editing

Good editing makes the difference between a poor newsletter and a good one, between a good publication and a great one.

SELECTING A NEWS STYLE

Once information is gathered, it must be written up in an appropriate news style. Approaches to writing news stories are straight reporting and features.

STRAIGHT REPORTING

The most common approach to writing a news story is straight reporting. Immediately, in the first sentence or first few sentences, the writer tells the reader the most important part of the story, the part that makes it news.

Terrence McQueeny has been named president of *The Kansas City Star and Times*, replacing Michael Davies, who retired after 27 years with the firm. McQueeny has been with the *Star-Times* for 17 years, the past five as first vice president.

The following paragraphs expand and document the information in the *lead* (the first paragraph).

The announcement was made following Tuesday's meeting of the *Star-Times* board of directors.

Davies, who is credited with building the *Star-Times* into a multinational conglomerate during his 11 years as president, had said six months ago that he would retire before the end of the year.

After being named president, McQueeny issued a statement saying that...

When all the essential information is on the page, the basic straight news story is complete. The story can stress any of the five Ws and H—who, what, where, when, why and how—though usually the who or what will be the most important.

FEATURE TREATMENT

The alternative to reporting news straight is writing a feature story. But how do you know when you have a feature story on your hands? There are several characteristics to look for. The chief characteristic of the feature story is that although it has a news peg, it is not, strictly speaking, news.

A news peg is the justification for a story, the element that is news or has recently been news. In the example above, the news peg is that McQueeny is the new president of the company. A story about McQueeny's long-time involvement with a local charity would be a feature.

What is played up in a feature story is not red-hot news but some element certain to be of interest to most readers. That element can be celebrity status, humor, tragedy, suspense or an extraordinary event. A feature may be pegged on what the writer knows is of ongoing interest or concern to readers, something like the space shuttle or unemployment or inflation.

The feature element may be present in the kind of handling the story lends itself to. Is there a lot of highly descriptive and colorful material in the story? Is it rich in ideas or in historic background and significance? Then it is probably right for feature treatment. Another form of feature story is the analysis or explanation of a complex event, which helps readers to a more thorough understanding of a situation from which the hard news arose.

Human Interest. Human interest stories are the most common of all feature story types. Their wide appeal is anchored firmly in most people's curiosity about other people's business success or personal lives. Traditionally, such stories relate an exceptional event in the life of an average citizen: a good deed performed or experienced; a strange encounter, with a happy ending.

The Time Element. Most newsletters are not issued daily; they come out weekly, monthly or even quarterly. Therefore the "news" in a newsletter is very likely the "olds." Events being reported may have happened two weeks, even two months ago.

Word of mouth, the daily newspaper, industry journals, bulletin board announcements or memos have already delivered the essential facts to most readers. They know the story. The newsletter may very well be retelling it. What is the proper approach, then?

The newsletter story must restate the essential facts to clarify and record the known news. But, because most readers already know the facts, the newsletter writer undertakes to spark interest by presenting the story in a feature treatment.

For this reason, it is actually more difficult to write for a newsletter than for a daily newspaper. In traditional newspaper work, if not in most contemporary news reporting, if you gave "just the facts, ma'am," you'd done your work. Reporting known news takes some more work; it also often provides opportunities to exercise some imagination and show off some interpretive skills. Newsletters offer opportunities for features.

Features are often fun to do. Consider the life of the sports writer for a newspaper. He must write about a game that happened the night before and that was reported by the evening news and radio. Most readers know who won and what the essential plays of the game were. Does he hang his head over his keyboard because there is nothing left for him? He does not.

Everything else is left for him. And, you may have noticed, newspaper sports stories are almost invariably more interesting than their electronic counterparts. The story may reveal the coach's magic (expletive deleted) words to the tight end just before he went in to catch a pass for the winning touchdown. Or it may describe how a team achieved victory under unknown handicaps.

The news peg for the sports writer is still the game. But there is, as people say, more to the game than who won. There is how the game was played. And the feature story can explore that *how* in detail, at some leisure. *Time is actually on the side of the feature story.*

The Delayed Lead. Feature stories usually take a delayed lead; that is, the facts of the story are not given right off. They are worked into the story, but the focus is on some detail or idea that is not the hard news focus. A feature story is to reporting what a close-up is to photography. The writer selects a certain element from the big picture and is able to give it a closer, more thorough and thoughtful look. A strong writer with an eye for detail thrives on this style of reporting.

One word of caution, however. A writer of limited gifts and skills may find that feature writing brings out the worst in him or her and may delay the lead until no reader can find it. If you are not sure of your skills, approach feature writing very gingerly, a little at a time, practicing and learning as you go what readers do and do not like.

WRITING THE INTERVIEW STORY

Writing the finished story from notes, you have two duties: (1) to be fair to the person interviewed and (2) to be considerate of the readers.

There will be a lot of repetition in any interview. Eliminate redundancies and repetition while running through notes seeking colorful and important quotes.

Similar quotes, or quotes on the same subject, may be widely separated in the interview. Pull them together to make the story more cohesive and easier for the reader to understand. Your obligation to the interviewee is not to say everything he said; it is to accurately represent what he said.

Where possible, paraphrase quotes into fewer, clearer words. Try to strike a happy balance between quoted material and paraphrase, without using too many paragraphs of either one all in a row. Alternate quotes and paraphrases.

You may start paragraphs with a quote and follow with the attributive, "she said." Avoid starting with "Jones said that. . ." Tell the reader what Jones said, then that Jones said it. But unless a quote is appropriate to key the reader to what the interview is about, a quote should not be used in the lead; a paraphrase is usually a better opening. But a good colorful quote is an ideal way to end a successful interview story.

THE ESSENTIAL STYLEBOOK

Every publication requires rules, commonly understood and written rules. A stylebook contains such rules for consistent style and usage. In any given publication, capitalization, for example, should be consistent. A publication that prints *Vice President* on one page and *vice president* on the next leads astute readers to suspect that such untidiness may extend to larger matters. If the writers cannot pay attention to such little details, then can they be trusted to get other things right, like the facts? In publishing, small inconsistencies affect credibility, even as in society at large a sloppy person's appearance affects his or her acceptance by some fastidious citizens.

A stylebook can include as few or as many rules as you think necessary. Some, e.g., *The University of Chicago Stylebook* and *The Associated Press Stylebook and Libel Manual*, are several hundred pages long.

A model stylebook is given in Appendix 2 of this book. It is brief, and it is offered to suggest what topics to consider in making decisions about your newsletter style. Readers will disagree with some of its directives. That's all right. Usage standards vary and are open to argument. But within any organization that publishes material, a guide to consistent usage is needed for all writers. A stylebook will prevent time loss to constant decision-making while writing. It will prevent time loss when a writer and an editor get into an argument over the appropriateness of semicolons for separating items in a series.

Some of the conventions covered in the model stylebook in the appendix are those for capitalization, punctuation, grammar, spelling, abbreviation and numbers. Conventions for abbreviations and numbers are especially troublesome.

Will you and other writers for your newsletter abbreviate state names in the old way, as Ariz., Calif., Miss., and Tenn.? Or will you use the postal service abbreviations AZ, CA, MS and TN? Either is acceptable, but a decision on one for consistent use is mandatory.

Should dates be abbreviated as in Jan. 6? Or do you prefer January 6? Decide.

In which usages will numbers be spelled out and in which will they be written as numerals? Will it be ten or 10? One million or 1,000,000? Fourteenth Street or 14th Street? Decide. Decide in all the cases of usage you can think of, and then write down the others as they come up and you make rulings on them.

Will a person's title and surname be used in second reference (Mr. Abernathy, Ms. Lewes)? Or will only the surname be used (Abernathy, Lewes)? This has been an unsettled issue and has taken some entertaining forms. One major daily got into terrible trouble with its readers when it printed a story about a convicted murderer, referring to him respectfully throughout the story by the title "Mr." After the outcry, the newspaper ceased to extend courtesy titles to murderers. Then Shana Alexander wrote a book about Jean Harris, the very ladylike woman who murdered Herman Tarnower, the doctor of Scarsdale diet fame. When the newspaper printed a review of the book, they referred throughout to "Ms. Alexander" and to "Harris."

Usage that involves a controversial issue may take some time to resolve. Should a female chairman be a chairwoman? A chair? Must men then be chairs too? This sometimes gets absurd. But these issues must be conscientiously faced and worked out. And then a decision must be made so that you can get on with the work at hand, which is to get the newsletter out.

When the basic decisions are made and circulated in writing, a stylesheet has been born. It will grow into a stylebook in its own time as controversies and questions arise and are resolved. Write decisions down the minute they are made, to avoid any future confusion.

Begin a list of words that cause recurrent trouble, whether with their spelling or their use. If "comprise" is included on your list as meaning what the whole does to the parts, never again does a writer on your staff spend ten minutes agonizing over whether the states comprise the Union or the Union comprises the states.

In short, having a stylebook means never having to say you're stymied by something stupidly small.

An agreed-upon dictionary, to be used as the final authority in usage, should be made available to all writers. *Webster's New World Dictionary* is the choice of many major dailies.

ELEMENTS OF NEWS WRITING

Good writing employs proper grammar and usage. It is clear, easy to read, and easy to understand. Good news writing has these features and several other distinguishing characteristics. They are as follows:

Accuracy in Facts and Spirit. Make every effort not only to establish the veracity of all information in a story, but also to assure that the total effect of the story is not misleading.

Check names and addresses carefully, using standard references such as telephone books, city directories and file clippings. Much information comes secondhand from newspapers and other media. Such data should be checked against basic sources. The more sources used, the greater the chance for accuracy.

When checking via telephone, exercise special care, because of the chance of misunderstanding. The letters *f* and *s*, for instance, sound similar. Ask that names be spelled out, using a verification system: *A as in Able, B as in Baker*, etc.

If you are still uncertain of a specific fact after checking more than one source, qualify the statement: *It is believed that...* (or) *Jones said he understood that...*

Even when you have verified all specific data, it is still possible to give the reader a false impression. Omission of one side of an issue or of an essential background fact can distort a story. Inadvertent comment and vague usage alike can mislead the reader. How old is an elderly man? A young one? Be specific.

Attribution of an emotional attitude to a person being quoted is another problem. Words like "demands," "denies," or "denounces" have strong meanings, and they attribute strong feelings to the speaker. "Said" is safe and neutral. There is nothing wrong with using it repeatedly. Avoid choosing strong words only for the sake of variation or color. Choose them only if they are the right words.

Be careful of assumptions and conclusions. If they are someone else's, attribute them. State the facts accurately and let readers draw their own conclusions.

Short Sentences & Paragraphs. News writing serves the reader who is in a hurry. The reader wants the facts: specific places, names, numbers, dates and events. The extra adjective or adverb is out of place in news writing. As a rule, limit sentences to fewer than 10 to 20 words and to one idea. Use active, not passive voice because active voice is concise and vigorous. Write that Eric Jones made the motion, not that the motion was made by Eric Jones.

A good length for a paragraph is two or three sentences, which is not what you learned in freshman English. But the object of an essay written in an English class is to develop a theme or an idea thoroughly. The object of news writing is to get the news to readers. Long paragraphs set in type in a narrow newsletter column would seem impenetrable to the reader. They are, in fact, difficult to read. Keep them short and simple.

Another virtue of short paragraphs is their flexibility. Often new information must be added to a story, or part of the story must be cut to make the story fit available space. A story constructed of short paragraphs makes either of these tasks easier to do without rewriting whole paragraphs.

Short Phrases & Words. Tell the story in the fewest words possible. It is harder to write, but easier to read. Look for unnecessary words in circumlocutions like the following.

arrived at the conclusion	concluded
at the present time *or*	
at this point in time	now

Decide if your notes contain a single most important news element or if there are several that are of nearly equal importance.

As you weigh these factors, keep in mind that *where* and *when* are seldom of top importance, though they can, indeed, sometimes be the most newsworthy element. (The accident happened on the way to the wedding. The baby was born in a pool hall.)

Why, i.e., the cause, reason or purpose, and *how*, i.e., the means by which, will sometimes be the most interesting points.

But usually, the *what* or the *who* is the real news of the story. The *who* is almost always newsworthy in a small circulation newsletter whose readers know everyone in the organization and like to read about them. The important part of the story will sometimes be a combination of these two—*who* did *what* or *what* happened to *whom*.

The trick to good lead writing is to immediately focus on this most newsworthy point of the story and to reserve other details until later in the story. Try to reduce the essence of the news to a single sentence or even a single word.

Try this simple device. Pretend you are calling a friend to report the news. You might start: "Do you know what happened?" "No, what happened?" Your answer to that question, "The board just voted to give us a 15 percent travel allowance increase," is your lead, essentially. At least it is the lead content.

Once you have decided what information should go into the lead, it still must be written in the most attention-getting way possible. Is there an especially interesting or unusual way to phrase the information? Is there a colorful word that can be put into the lead? Is there a dramatic or humorous element to the story?

The lead takes two basic forms: the *direct lead* and the *delayed lead*.

The direct lead conveys immediacy and gets right to the point. It can touch on a single news element, combine two news elements or summarize several elements such as the results of a meeting. It is important to avoid putting too much in the lead. Do not confuse the reader with too much information all at once.

Here is a snappy single-point lead:

Local bicyclists will ride more safely on our streets starting today, thanks to a new bikeway system just approved by the city council.

Here is a lead burdened with too much information:

Ted Burns, Mary McCleary and Robert Day, members of our congregation, all suffered minor injuries when the car they share in a car pool skidded on ice as they were driving to church and collided with a car driven by Ruth Ann Schull at 10th and Washington Streets shortly before 11 a.m. Sunday, according to Sheriff Mike Kindinger.

Documentation, clarification, authority and additional details can be saved for the paragraphs following the lead. In the example here the essential news is that three church members who shared rides were injured on their way to church. Other information should be delayed until the paragraphs following the lead.

The delayed lead takes a more roundabout approach than the direct lead. It uses several sentences to set up a background or explain the context for a reflective mood story. It employs suspense to capture the readers' attention and then leads them to the newsworthy outcome.

Delayed leads start with a teaser, an interesting side issue, and then work to the central news point. They arouse anticipation rather than thrusting the news straight at the reader.

Like all municipal officials, Mayor Terry Wood of Outback, Missouri, is faced with a tight budget.

And like other officials, he needs to meet the demands of the citizens of his community for services like park and street maintenance. To do so, he needs, among other things, a pickup truck. But money for a truck is not in the Outback budget.

So the mayor called the Mid-America Regional Council, which coordinates the distribution of excess government property for the region. Staff members checked a catalog issued monthly by the state and found a 1966 Dodge cargo pickup truck listed. The truck was located at the Defense Property Disposal Office in Columbus, Ohio.

Forms were filled out, and soon the truck belonged to Outback.

The only hitch: Wood had to pick it up and drive it back to Outback.

In the past six months, MARC has helped distribute $350,000 worth of equipment...

The story goes on to list equipment distributed, and it ends with the two oddest requests—for a railroad locomotive and some baseball equipment.

For both direct and delayed leads, every conceivable rhetorical device has been used: contrast, question, literary allusion, parody, quotation, dialogue, figurative speech, direct address, epigram and description.

Any number of different leads could properly be used on the same story. With experience, writers quickly find the right opening. When a lead feels right, a story will sometimes unfold easily, telling itself the rest of the way.

A good lead catches the reader's attention, whether the story is long or short, straight news or feature, analysis or background.

WRITING THE BODY

Short Items & Stories. For very short stories, the body may be a single sentence or paragraph documenting the lead. A surprise punch ending is effective in short shorts.

A new membership directory has been published for members of the American Rural Electric Association (*the lead*). It is available for the asking from the national office; write or call for your copy (*the body*).

Jim Garrity, who chaired the committee that planned the annual company picnic last month, anticipated every problem except one (*the lead*). He broke his leg the day before the picnic and was unable to attend (the *body*).

Short shorts come in handy. They enable an editor to cover a large amount of news in brief form. The same is true for the reader. Short shorts are much in demand when an editor begins laying out pages; they fill small holes in the page and, when boxed with a rule, enhance page layout.

Longer News Stories. The body of the traditional longer news story usually takes one of three forms: (1) inverted pyramid, (2) chronological or (3) structured.

Inverted pyramid. The inverted pyramid form requires a writer to confine separate blocks of information to paragraphs; these paragraphs are arranged by importance, the most important early in the story, the least important toward the end.

Readers get the most important information first and can stop reading when they have learned as much as they want to know, before the end of the story. Furthermore, in laying out a page using stories written in this form, the editor can drop paragraphs from the bottom to make copy that is too long fit the space available, knowing that essential information will not be lost.

Chronological. Organizing a story chronologically is not only natural for the writer to write, it is natural for the reader to read. After the lead, the writer merely tells the rest of the story in the sequence in which the events happened. Art imitates nature in the very simplest way in chronological writing.

Structured. The structured form, as a rule, builds to a climax, keeping the reader in suspense. It captures the reader's attention, intertwines documentation, authority and facts throughout the body, and leads the reader to a conclusion, often with a surprise ending. It cannot be cut indiscriminately without leaving the reader hanging.

MAKING A TWO-STORY STORY

Sometimes it is difficult to weave in important collateral information with the main news thread of a story. One device is to write two stories—the main news story and a *sidebar*, a second story containing the related information. This not only leaves the two separate but closely related stories clear and distinct, but also brightens up a page layout of otherwise "gray" text.

Frequently the second, sidebar story is an illustrative feature on the same subject as a general news story. For example, if a record heat wave is the subject of a general news story, then a feature sidebar might contain the story of how one resourceful person is fighting off the heat.

Another use is to break out statistics from a main story that is heavily laden with numbers, and run them in a table in a box adjacent to the story. As writers, most of us assume that the best way to give people information is with words. Information graphics such as pie charts and graphs are often more successful at conveying information than words.

PageMaker King in Newsletter Publishing

Lorem ipsum dolor sit amet, con secteteur adipsicing elit, sed diam nonnumy nibh euisnod tempor inci dunt ut labore et dolore magna ali quam erat volupat.

Ut wise enim ad minim veniam, quis nostrud exerci tation ullamcorper suscipit laboris nisl ut aliquip ex ea commodo con sequat. Duis autem vel eum irure dolor in henderit in vulputate velit esse consequat.

Vel illum dolor eu feugiat mulla facilsi at vero eos et accusm et ius to odio dignessim qui blandt prae sent

as minim veniam, quis nostrud exerci tation ullamcorper suscipit laboris nisl ut aliquip ex ea commodo sonsequat. Dues atuem velit esse mol estie consequat.

Hanc ego cum tene senteniam, quid est cur verear ne ad eam non possing accommodare nost ros quos tu apule ante cum memorite tum etia ergat. Facile erricerd possit duo conetud notier si effercerit, et opes bel fortuanag vel ingen liberalitat magis conveniunt, da but tuntung ben evolent sib concillant, et aptis sim est ad quite.

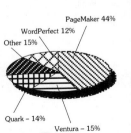

Not all of your readers are "word" oriented. Consider graphics that present information visually.

PageMaker King in Newsletter Publishing

Lorem ipsum dolor sit amet, con secteteur adipsicing elit, sed diam nonnumy nibh euisnod tempor inci dunt ut labore et dolore magna ali quam erat volupat.

Ut wise enim ad minim veniam, quis nostrud exerci tation ullamcorper suscipit laboris nisl ut aliquip ex ea commodo con sequat. Duis autem vel eum irure dolor in henderit in vulputate velit esse consequat.

Vel illum dolor eu feugiat mulla facilis at vero eos et accusm et ius to odio dignessim qui blandt prae sent luptatum zzril delenit aigue duos dolore et mosestias excepteur sint occaecat cupidtat not simil pro vident tempor sunt in culpa qui officia desrunt mollit aniom ib est abor un et dolor fuga.

Et harumd dereud facilis est er expedit distint. Nam liber tempor cum soluta nobis eligent option congue nibil impediet doming id quod maxim plecat facer possum omnis voluptas assumenda est, mnis repellend.

Temporibud auteui quinsud et aur offik debit aut tum rerum necessit atib saepe evenit ut er mosit non recusand. Itaque earun rerum hic ten tury sapiente delectus au aut perfer zim edndis dolorib asperiore repellat. Hanc ego cum teme senteniam, quid est kur verear ne ad eam non possing accommodare nost ros quos tu paulo ante cum emmorite tum etia ergat. Nos amice et nbevol, olestias access potest fier ad augent ascum consci ent to factor tum poen legum odio qui civiumda. Et tamen in busdam negque nonor imper.

Nos amice et memorite tum etia ergat mbevp. Pestoas aces est foer ad aigend ascum consci ent to factor tum ppoen legum odio que civiuna. Et tamen in busdam neque

as minim veniam, quis nostrud exerci tation ullamcorper suscipit laboris nisl ut aliquip ex ea commodo sonsequat. Dues atuem velit esse mol estie consequat.

Hanc ego cum tene senteniam, quid est cur verear ne ad eam non possing accommodare nost ros quos tu apule ante cum memorite tum etia ergat. Facile erricerd possit duo conetud notier si effercerit, et opes bel fortuanag vel ingen liberalitat magis conveniunt, da but tuntung ben evolent sib concillant, et aptis sim est ad quite.

Vel illum dolor eu feugiat mulla facilis at vero eos et accusm et ius to odio dignessim qui blandt prae sent luptatum zzril delenit aigue duos dolore et mosestias excepteur sint occaecat cupidtat not simil pro vident tempor sunt in culpa qui officia desrunt mollit aniom ib est abor un et dolor fuga. Et harumd dereud facilis est er expedit distint. Nam liber tempor cum soluta.

Software Checklist for Editors

- ☑ changes column widths to support grids
- ☑ contains built-in spell checker
- ☑ supports spot color
- ☑ prints pages in printer spreads
- ☑ imports graphics easily
- ☑ supports common graphic file types
- ☑ allows control of halftone screens
- ☑ creates drop caps automatically

QuarkXPress Gains Ground

Vel illum dolor eu feugiat mulla facilis at vero eos et accusm et ius to odio dignessim qui blandt prae sent luptatum zzril delenit aigue duos dolore et mosestias excepteur sint occaecat cupidtat not simil pro vident tempor sunt in culpa qui officia desrunt mollit aniom ib est abor un et dolor fuga.

Et harumd dereud facilis est er expedit distint. Nam liber tempor cum soluta nobis eligent option congue nibil impediet doming id quod maxim plecat facer possum omnis voluptas assumenda est, mnis repellend.

Temporibud auteui quinsud et aur offik debit aut tum rerum

necessit atib saepe evenit ut er mosit non recusand. Itaque earun rerum hic ten tury sapiente delectus au aut perfer zim edndis dolorib asperiore repellat. Hanc ego cum teme senteniam, quid est kur verear ne ad eam non possing accommodare nost ros quos tu paulo ante cum emmorite tum etia ergat. Nos amice et nbevol, olestias access potest fier ad augent ascum consci ent to factor tum poen legum odio qui civiumda. Et tamen in busdam negque nonor imper.

Vel illum dolor eu feugiat mulla facilsi at vero eos et accusm et ius to odio dignessim qui blandt prae sent luptatum zzri.

Sidebars break out information from long articles. They also help dress up the page design.

7 Tips for Professional Speed

Not too far into your career as a newsletter writer you are going to yearn for newspaper experience. You will long to know how editors and writers of daily newspapers spew out high-quality material under tight deadline.

Here are seven tips from professional journalists to help get you up to professional speed.

1. Before you collect content, sit down and determine the fastest way to get the information you need. Collect as much as possible by phone or fax or through the mail, including e-mail.
2. Don't over-research. Collect only what you need and don't get sidetracked by other interesting information.
3. If an article seems too complicated or research gets too involved, simplify the theme of the article. Break it into several articles.
4. Organize the strongest points of the article before you start to write and outline it.
5. Write the rough draft as quickly as possible without fretting over the lead or polishing sentences.
6. Go back through the article and fill in the details, strengthen the verbs.
7. Write to fit the word count assigned to the piece.

Rewriting a Story

The first draft of a story is seldom the best. There are holes to be filled, authority to be added, wording to be improved, and meaning to be clarified. "Get it down," said Hemingway, "then get it right." To get it right, rewrite.

Read the first draft. Have someone else read it. Make corrections, compare it with notes, look for ways to sharpen, brighten and improve the story. Check facts, shorten sentences, remove unnecessary and inaccurate qualifiers, rewrite phrases and sentences. On the computer a quick search can be made for overused qualifiers such as *just* and *very* and for over-anxious ones such as *terribly* and *vastly*. Many adverbs meant to intensify meaning diminish meaning instead. Try (just) reading your sentences with and without such qualifiers, and you will see how (terribly) often they are (very vastly) stronger without the extra baggage. (Search for *ly* and see what you see...)

Check spelling and punctuation against the stylebook. Recheck names, addresses and figures. Make sure that facts are documented and authorities are given.

Look at the lead. Does it contain enough information? Is too much crammed into it?

Read the draft out loud. It is easy to skip obvious errors when reading silently. A sentence may look all right but, when read aloud, may not read smoothly and logically. If a sentence or phrase isn't clear, rephrase it.

You may be writing all of the content of your newsletter yourself. Or, perhaps you have submissions from others so that you now have the tricky job of editing. Most likely, you are doing both.

EDITORS ALL OVER THE PLACE

On large newspapers, completed stories go to managing editors, news editors and city editors who judge them for relative news value. The editors decide what length to run stories and where to place them; they write the headlines and captions. Stories are then funneled to a copy desk where copy editors proofread and verify their facts. There are editors all over the place.

But on smaller publications, often only one editor performs all these functions.

Good editing makes the difference between a poor newsletter and a good one, between a good publication and a great one. Good editing also enhances page design and layout. Here's how to approach the task of thorough editing.

A CHECKLIST FOR EDITORS

When you go over a story, you will be doing many jobs at once:

- ❏ Read a story through quickly, sizing it up for content and relative news value.
- ❏ Correct obvious errors of fact or spelling.
- ❏ Check the story for conformity to stylebook rules.
- ❏ Rewrite the lead if necessary.
- ❏ Break long paragraphs into shorter ones.
- ❏ Add subheads to longer articles.
- ❏ Decide if the story is too long for its relative news worth and, if so, trim it. If it is incomplete or too skimpy for the import of the news it has to tell, round it out or, if possible, have the original writer do so.
- ❏ Go over the story carefully, looking for mistakes in punctuation, grammar and facts. Recheck facts, especially names, addresses, numbers and titles.
- ❏ Watch for potentially libelous statements; make sure the story is accurate and that it represents fairly all sides of an issue.
- ❏ Write the headline.
- ❏ Write captions, pull quotes and other text that will be given special treatment in the layout.

As you polish the story, look for the elements of good news writing: conciseness, clarity, accuracy and vigor. Cut unnecessary words and phrases, tighten loose writing, rephrase jumbled or confused sentence structure, substitute concise verbs for vague ones, change the general to the specific.

Look for hidden leads. Is the real news buried? If so, pull it up and write a new lead. (Hint: you'll often find the best lead sentence buried three paragraphs down into the article.)

Do not make changes, however, for no reason. It is not enough that you would have written the story differently than the writer did. Preserve the special approach and flavor of the writer's style.

This, basically, is what a copy editor does. But the news writer/ copy editor/editor often has a special problem. You may have written many of the stories yourself.

EDITING WITH GRAMMAR CHECKERS

Editing your own copy is risky. You are apt to overlook the mistakes you made when you wrote it. It is difficult to see the story from a new perspective. Let some time elapse before you edit your own stories, so that they won't be so close. Tackle them with the critical eye and objectivity you would use on other writers' stories. Be tough on your work.

If you have access to a word processor, learn to use it. Features like spell-checking, thesauruses, cut-and-paste editing and grammar-checking can make your editing job easier.

Note: don't rely solely on your spelling checker (also called a *spell-check*) for proofreading. It won't catch errors such as *that* when you meant to type *than*, and it often encourages you to replace words it doesn't know with amusing substitutes, such as *pacemaker* for *PageMaker*.

But if possible, avoid editing your own stories. Perhaps there are others on your staff who can edit your stories. If you are a one-person operation, turn elsewhere for help. A top secretary could proofread your story for grammar, punctuation and spelling. An executive in another department could check it for facts and overall content.

And there is nothing wrong with having the source of a story check it for accuracy—except that it may be sent back written in some ponderous, non-news style. Make it clear in advance that you don't want the story rewritten, that you want it read only for overall accuracy. (Some editors attach a short instruction sheet explaining exactly what they want checked. Others highlight numbers, names and quotes, and note "please verify highlighted information for accuracy." Many editors notice fewer rewrites when articles are submitted for checking in layout form rather than double-spaced text.)

Find the most talented editing help you can. Even among trained journalists, top copy editors are hard to find. Ideally, they are knowledgeable, skeptical, principled, irreverent, artistic and talented. They have a sense of humor, take the job seriously, and do not make changes for the sake of change. Yet they take nothing for granted. They question facts, names and grammar—and they check them against references: dictionary, telephone book, city directory, world almanac and stylebook.

Copy editors keep the spirit of the story, but at the same time they organize, brighten, correct and polish it. They leave a story much better than they find it.

Chapter 7

Secret Formulas
for Headlines

*Nothing distinguishes a professional
newsletter from an amateur one so quickly
as the quality of the headlines.*

THE IMPORTANCE OF GOOD HEADLINES

Nothing distinguishes a professional newsletter from an amateur one so quickly as the quality of the headlines. Because headlines are prominent, the reader's eye goes to them first. Over half of the recipients of your newsletter will read the headlines. In the first few seconds of scanning, the reader's crucial first impression of the publication is formed. The importance of taking the time and effort to write and edit good headlines cannot be overstated.

Well-written headlines distill the essence of the news point of a story. They are positive and specific; they contain strong, active verbs and short, simple words.

Writing good headlines takes practice and study. Spend some time with a good newspaper, studying the headlines in it. Headline writers on large newspapers are often among the most talented and experienced people on the staff. They become specialists in headline writing because they have a seasoned, almost instinctive, understanding of the essence of a news story. They write headlines hour after hour, day after day; for this reason, they excel at writing headlines.

In contemporary headline writing, unfortunately, there is a trend toward the "cute" headline. Puns are widely used by formerly sedate newspapers. Some of the uses are better than others. Examples of this breed of humorous headline are: *Bjorn Again!* (when Bjorn Borg won a tennis tournament) and *State money woes/Give hospital pain.* (We admired the former, regretted the latter.)

So many major metropolitan dailies use puns so relentlessly in headlines now that one suspects something is up, that their market research divisions have announced that puns sell papers. However, some great newspapers that, as of this writing, do not use puns in headlines are *The New York Times, The Washington Post* and *The Philadelphia Bulletin.*

In addition to studying professionally written headlines, spend some time learning the classic journalistic rules for writing good ones. Review these rules (see *15 Ways to Write Good Headlines* below) before each headline writing session.

WHAT AN ARRESTING HEADLINE DOES

Gets Attention. The first function of a good headline is to get the reader's attention. That's why it is printed in larger type than the text. That's why its few words must be so carefully chosen.

Tells the Story. A good headline tells readers what a story is about. It induces them to read the story. Even if they don't, however, they can catch the essence of a story from a well-written headline. Readers should be able to pick up the main news in a newsletter by scanning only its headlines.

Leads the Reader Into the Story. Successful headlines do more than tell the story. They capture the readers' interest and make them want to read on.

Classifies the Story. The size and style of a headline give readers some idea of the importance of the story. They show the relation of the story to others in the newsletter. The bigger the head and the more prominence it is given on a page, the more important the story.

Enhances the Page. The typography and style of a headline work to enhance the appearance of a page. Headlines work together on a page to present a lively and interesting face, to form attractive patterns as well as to tell the news.

WHAT AN ATTENTION-GRABBING HEADLINE SAYS

The headline is often taken from the lead. The main news in a properly written straight news story is in the lead, which may run for several sentences or even several paragraphs. The headline writer sifts through them, pinpoints the news, and forms a story sentence—a sentence that sums up the main news point of the story.

For example, assume a story is about the hiring of five new teachers by a school district for the coming year. The story sentence would be: school district hires five new teachers for 1995-96 term.

The headline would feature the key words of that sentence: five teachers hired.

Then, depending on the amount of space allotted for the head, it would include such other information as the term they were hired for and who hired them. This kind of headline is relatively easy to write.

A story that comprises various facts may need a general headline. Say an agency has reorganized. It previously was divided into five departments. One new department has been added and two of the former five departments have merged.

The main news point is not that a new department has been added or that two other departments have been combined. The main news point is that there has been a major reorganization.

To single out only one of the points would not tell the whole story. The headline writer would focus on the reorganization and its expected result.

How Headlines Fail

Many newsletter headlines not only fail to focus on the main news point but also rely on words too general or too vague to give the reader the gist of the story. There are several categories of headlines to avoid.

The Label Head. An organization forms a new volunteer league. The headline reads: *Volunteer League.* Volunteer League what? Readers, if they have the time and patience, must read the story to find that a new league was formed to organize and train volunteers and that they are being urged to join it. The headline, at the very least, should tell readers that.

The Question Head. Another kind of head that falls short of doing its job is the question head: *Is the Transit Plan Working?* Readers may be interested enough to read the story to find out the answer. But the headline space might be better used to tell readers why the plan is working, if it is.

The Vague Head. Another failed headline is the "meeting held" variety. The headline *Committee Meets* tells readers next to nothing. What did the committee do? What's the news?

The How or Why Head. The how or why headline is a little better: *How Stock Options Work.* This at least holds out a promise to readers and may even tempt them to read the story. But it communicates no concrete information.

The Clever Head. A clever headline may work for some feature stories—those that involve humor, suspense or extraordinary events or that are highly descriptive. But a good, clever headline is more than just clever; it captures what any good news headline does: key words, color, vitality, specific images and the essential news.

Alliteration, puns and rhymes seldom work the way you want them to. If you suspect that a headline employing one of these conventions will evoke groans rather than smiles from your newsletter audience, rewrite it in a more conventional form. Occasionally allusion, irony, wit, metaphors, catch phrases, labels, questions and captions work in feature headlines. It is all right to break the rules and try one of these devices occasionally for a feature story.

Good headlines, whether on straight news or features, bring focus to a story and announce it with flair and action.

15 WAYS TO WRITE GOOD HEADLINES

1. **Use Active Voice.** The dynamic active voice saves words. *Man Bites Dog* is livelier than *Dog Is Bitten By Man.* The subject and verb act as one. Also, the passive voice costs extra words and often makes a headline too long to fit the space available for it. Use the passive voice, however, if the active voice will delay the essential news. *Pay Hike OKd By Board* puts the real subject, the core news, first, as *Board OKs Pay Hike* does not.

2. **Use Present Tense.** To convey a feeling of immediacy, write headlines in the present tense, even if
the story reports something that happened in the
recent past. Write *Robber Flees* rather than *Robber
Fled*. Use the infinitive or future tense to announce
a future event. *Lawyers To Debate Insanity Plea*.

3. **Use Short, Pithy Words.** Use short synonyms for long
words. Panel or group will more likely fit into a headline than will committee. Furthermore, long words can
obscure meaning. *Work Begins On Broadway Bridge*
communicates more than does *Bridge Repair Plan
Implemented*. Adjectives are seldom needed in headlines, and there is seldom room for them.

4. **Avoid "To Be" Verbs.** Headline writers delete
helping verbs such as *is* and *are*. This omission saves
space and punches up the headline. *Physicians Asked To
Staff Clinic* omits the understood helping verb *are*.

5. **Make Positive Statements.** State negative information in positive form. *No Action Taken On Ruling By
Pacifists* would be better written *Pacifists Decline to
Act on Ruling*. This construction also avoids confusion about who made the ruling. The pacifists did
not make the ruling, yet the first headline makes it
appear that they did.

6. **Be Specific.** Use precise words. *Editor Named Employee-of-the-Month* communicates a more concrete
idea than does *Woman Named Employee-of-the-
Month*. If readers know the editor, write *Janice
Wright Named Employee-of-the-Month*. Headlines
that name a person work especially well with a
photo of the person.

   General words and vague words make dull headlines. One of the deadest headlines is the *standing
head*, the "Message from the President." Write a live

headline about the president's message; tell readers what the president has on his or her mind. Then maybe they'll read the column.

Being specific does not include putting insignificant or outdated matter in a headline. The specific date, for instance, does not matter much after an event. The reader's first response is to think he or she has missed something.

7. **Be Accurate.** A headline that sums up a speech must include attribution. Don't write *Inflation Rate To Slow Down* as though it were a fact. Part of the news is who says so. Write *Inflation Will Slow, Kemp Says*.

8. **Be Impartial.** Watch words that color a headline's meaning or reflect the writer's opinion. Words like *denies* or *claims* have connotations that may misrepresent the facts. *Rose Lashes Board's Action* may overstate Rose's criticism.

9. **Don't Repeat Key Words.** *Committee Ousts Committee Chairman* is unacceptable. Look for synonyms; find another way to phrase the headline. *Committee Ousts Its Chairman*.

10. **Avoid Confusing Line-Divisions.** Don't divide hyphenated words or words that go together from one line to the next. *Group Votes To/Renew Plea.* Here the split infinitive can be avoided by reworking the head: *Group Votes/To Renew Plea.*

11. **Omit Articles.** Generally, the articles *a, an* and *the* are omitted to improve action and to save space.

12. **Avoid Abbreviations.** *Salesman Wins Trip To LV.* Readers may not catch on that LV is Las Vegas.

13. **Avoid Exclamation Points & Other Punctuation.** In almost all instances, exclamation points don't have the effect you want—they squeak like adolescent cheerleaders instead of commanding attention

like good broadcasters. Replace exclamation points with strong, accurate verbs. Replace periods with semicolons and double quotes with single quotes. Use commas sparingly, though the comma is often used in place of *and* in headlines.

14. **Use Important Numbers Only.** Except for *one*, numbers in headlines should be written as numerals: *23 Leave Camp for Wilderness.* Dollar amounts are often meaningless unless they are compared to other figures: *$100,000 Added to Cost of Bridge* may be insignificant if the bridge costs $4 million, or it may be important if the bridge costs $200,000.

15. **Avoid Contrived Headlines.** Puns, rhymes, and alliteration are seldom appropriate in headlines.

A good list of short headline words is available in the book *Headlines and Deadlines* by Robert E. Garst and Theodore M. Bernstein. Such a list provides short synonyms for long words and is a valuable tool for making headlines fit.

Chapter 8

Editing for Design

*The editor's final job in improving the copy
is to look ahead to the layout stage.*

EDITING FOR VISUALLY-EFFECTIVE DESIGN

Since writing and layout are usually done in two distinct steps, many editors and writers must understand how the words they write affect the page layout. Effective editing creates a word/design synergy.

What makes for good news writing makes for good news design. Design-critical wording includes short paragraphs, short leads, short articles, articles beginning and ending on the same page and sub-heads included in long articles. Encourage contributors to write visual guides such as subheads. List word counts for them as part of your style guide.

The editor's final job in improving the copy is to look ahead to the layout stage. If you know ahead of time the typographical treatment an article will receive—kickers, decks, captions and pull quotes—you can write the text for the typographical treatments along with the copy for the rest of the article.

LETTING READERS COME UP FOR AIR

While you want variety in paragraph length, try to keep paragraphs four sentences or shorter. This lends "breathing room" to the columns of text in the newsletter. Hitting the return key more often is one of the easiest ways to improve the look of most newsletter text.

One widely accepted defining characteristic of a newsletter is that it has three or four articles per page. With the exception of some feature stories, the articles in your newsletter must be *short*. To achieve three or four articles per page, the length of your articles will be roughly between 250 and 300 words.

The way you type your newsletter text into the computer also affects the design. Spacing twice after periods adds unsightly gaps to the text. Encourage writers to space only once after a period. (If you can't break yourself or your writers of this "typewriting" habit, use the search and replace function on your word processor. Replace all occurrences of two spaces with one.)

Newsletter News 7

Clear Up Muddy Copyright Waters

Copyright law confuses many newsletter editors. Heck, it boggles many lawyers, so don't feel bad. Copyright law protects words or graphic images as the property of the person who created them. While it protects the means used to express an idea, it does not guard the idea itself.

This means that you can cull information from magazines, write it in your own words and be freed from copyright violation. Industry ethics say that you should credit the information source. The same goes for cartoons or illustrations. You can be inspired by a cartoon, redraw it (not just tracing), change the caption and be freed of copyright violation. Ethically you should also list the source of inspiration. Many people mistakenly think a work is not copyrighted if it isn't accompanied by the "©" symbol. Not so. Every idea put into a tangible form—ink, paper, magnetic tape, digital disk—is copyrighted.

Some editors justify reprinting materials by saying its for teaching purposes only. That falls under "fair use" exceptions of copyright law, right? Nope. Fair use exceptions state that you may quote briefly from a copyrighted work without asking permission for purposes of criticism, comment, news reporting, teaching, or research. The amount you quote can't be a substantial portion of the copyrighted work.

These two criteria are not clear cut. The interpretation of your newsletter's purpose and what constitutes a "substantial portion" is left up to a judge to decide. "Protection under fair use is so limited that you shouldn't take solace that you'll be protected by it," says lawyer Brian Smith of Brian L. Smith & Associates.

Also, while an informative newsletter could be considered news reporting, it's being published for marketing purposes and direct financial gain (hopefully) and isn't protected by these exceptions. If you forge ahead and quote a copyrighted work, cite the title, publisher and publication date. Of interest to any researcher, works created by the U.S. government do not carry copyright protection.

Here are some items commonly reprinted in newsletters along with tips on how to track down the copyright owner and ask for permission. If you wish to reprint a cartoon, write for permission. Most owners charge a fee. If your newsletter is a free publication, state this in your letter of request as it may lower or remove the fee. Some cartoons are available in clip art collections.

Clip art collections are copyrighted. Clip art publishers grant buyers a license to reprint the art but these rights vary dramatically by collection. Some licenses specify use only in free publications or those under a certain circulation. Read the rights carefully before you buy.

Yep. Copyrighted, too. Poems and lyrics are probably the items the most frequently reprinted without permission. It's hard to track down the author of an unsigned or anonymous poem. Even if it is signed, finding the poet may be next to impossible. Quoting a stanza or even a few lines of a song is an infringement of the owners copyright. Lyrics are considered sheet music and the rights are held by the music publisher. To find the publisher, look on the disc or tape or call BMI, ASCAP or CESAC. These companies have offices in Nashville, New York and Los Angeles.

To be on the save side, you must get permission to quote even a brief sentence or two from an article. You don't need permission if you use the articles as background research that you then write up entirely in your own words. If a letter is addressed to the editor, there's implied permission to reprint; however, that's more by custom than by law. All letters are protected by copyright law. Most editors call for verbal approval to reprint any letter.

With the widespread availability of scanners is awfully tempting to simply scan photos or art, change it a bit and reprint it. Write for permission or use something else. Also, obtain a model release from any person appearing in the photographs you use. Though photographers own the copyrights to the photos they create, people appearing in the photos have rights, too.

Quotations are covered under copyright protection. However, few, if any, publications write the person for permission to reprint.

It shocks most editors to find out that the work they pay subcontractors $50 to $150 per hour to create is actually owned by the subcontractor. In the absence of an agreement stating otherwise, you have only one-time usage rights. If you want com-

plete rights to a subcontractor's work, you need a copyright release which spells this out. The work of employees of a company belongs to the company as a "work for hire" under U.S. copyright law.

The first issue of this newsletter contained an article about a stock illustration service called Laughing Stock. The headline mistakenly read "Clip Art With an Attitude." One of the first responses back on the newsletter was a letter from Laughing Stock saying "NO! We do not provide clip art. We are a stock illustration agency." Stock illustration is ordered on a fee for use basis.

Pages 134 and 176 of *Marketing With Newsletters* say that most clip art is public domain. Martha LaFleur of WordPro Communication Design wrote to say, "Most clip art is NOT public domain." Public domain is when the copyright on a work has expired and its up for grabs by anyone. Under current law, this is the author's life plus 50 years for works created by an individual. The publishers of clip art retain copyright control and sell limited usage to buyers, not complete ownership.

It's worth it to pay special attention to copyright issues. Under current law, statutory damages of between $500 and $100,000 per infringement plus court costs and attorney's fees as set by the judge. You also pay in lost time, headaches and loss of face.

Okay, let's be realistic for a moment. Are newsletter editors going to quote a line of a song or reprint a cartoon from time to time without asking for permission? Of course. Limited circulation newsletters, such as those passed out to residents of a nursing home, take very little risk in doing so and hands of writing for permission for every item just isn't worth avoiding the risk.

However, the deeper the pockets of your organization and the larger the newsletter circulation, the greater the risk you take. A disgruntled employee may sue you for not getting a model release of your marketing department may insert your newsletter into a press kit and send it to the author of the article you reprinted without permission. It's best to know the risk you're taking beforehand (though you'll plead ignorance if trouble arises) and weigh them against the work of obtaining permission.

MANAGEMENT

Clear Up Muddy Copyright Waters

A quick swim through how copyright law affects newsletters

Copyright law confuses many newsletter editors. Heck, it boggles many lawyers, so don't feel bad.

Copyright law protects words or graphic images as the property of the person who created them. A work doesn't have to be accompanied by the "©" symbol to be protected.

While it protects the means used to express an idea, it does not guard the idea itself. This means that you can cull information from magazines, write it in your own words and be freed from copyright violation. Industry ethics say that you should credit the source.

Fair usage laws—safe water?
Fair use exceptions state that you may quote briefly from a copyrighted work without asking permission for purposes of criticism, news reporting, teaching, or research. The amount you quote can't be a substantial portion. These two criteria are not clear cut. The interpretation of your newsletter's purpose and what constitutes a "substantial portion" is left up to a judge to decide. "Protection under fair use is so limited that you shouldn't take solace that you'll be protected by it," says lawyer Brian Smith of Brian L. Smith & Associates.

If you forge ahead and quote a copyrighted work, cite the title, publisher and publication date. Works created by the U.S. government do not carry copyright protection.

Specific concerns for newsletters
Here are some items commonly reprinted in newsletters along with tips on how to track down the copyright owner.

Cartoons. If you wish to reprint a cartoon, write for permission. Most owners charge a fee. If your newsletter is a free publication, state this in your letter of request as it may lower the fee.

Lyrics. Quoting even a few lines of a song is an infringement of the owners' copyright. The rights are held by the music publisher. Poems and lyrics are probably the items most frequently infringed upon.

News articles. To be on the safe side, you must get permission to quote even a brief sentence or two from an article. You don't need permission if you paraphrase the material.

Letters. If a letter is addressed to the editor, there's implied permission to reprint; however, all letters are protected by copyright law. Most editors call the author for verbal approval.

Photographs & illustrations. Write for permission to reprint or scan. Also, obtain a model release from any person appearing in the photographs. Though photographers own the copyrights to the photos they create, people appearing in the photos have rights, too.

Quotations. Quotations are covered under copyright protection. However, few, if any, publications write for permission to reprint.

Subcontracted work. It shocks most editors to find out that work you pay writers and designers $50 to $150 per hour to create is actually owned by the subcontractor. In the absence of an agreement stating otherwise, you have one-time usage rights. For complete rights, you need a copyright release which spells this out.

Calming the waters
Okay, realistically speaking, are many newsletter editors going to quote a line of a song or reprint a cartoon from time to time without asking for permission? Of course.

Limited circulation newsletters, such as those passed out to residents of a nursing home, take very little risk in doing so.

However, the deeper the pockets of your organization and the larger the newsletter circulation, the greater the risk you take. Your newsletter may be placed into a press kit and sent to the author of the article you reprinted without permission.

It's best to know the risk you're taking beforehand (though you'll plead ignorance if trouble arises) and weigh them against the work of obtaining permission. ▪

> **A work doesn't have to be accompanied by the "©" symbol to be protected.**

Clip Art & Public Domain Defined

The first issue of this newsletter contained an article with the headline, "Clip Art With an Attitude." One of the first responses back on the newsletter was a letter from Laughing Stock saying "We do NOT provide clip art. We are a stock illustration agency." Stock illustration is ordered on a fee for use basis.

My book, *Marketing With Newsletters*, states that most clip art is public domain. Martha LaFleur of WordPro Communication Design wrote to say, "Most clip art is NOT public domain." Public domain is when the copyright on a work has expired and its up for grabs by anyone.

Clip art collections are copyrighted. The publishers grant buyers a license to reprint the art but these rights vary dramatically by collection. Some licenses specify use only in free publications or those under a certain circulation. Read the rights carefully.

Resources:
Brian L. Smith, Attorney & Counselor at Law; Nashville, TN: (615) 452-5282. For a free copy of **The Smith Report**, a newsletter on copyright and intellectual property, call or fax (615) 451-1033.
Martha LaFleur, WordPro Communication Design; (319) xxx-xxxx.

Notice the difference that short paragraphs, subheads, kickers, decks, pull quotes and sidebars make in the page design of the second example.

Another tip for achieving a professionally typeset look is to learn the keyboard strokes that change " " quotes (called *dumb quotes*) into " " quotes (called *smart quotes*). You can buy a software utility that automatically changes the quote style for you.

WRITING KICKERS & DECKS

Glance back at the section *What an Arresting Headline Does*. Those are a lot of tasks for a one- or two-line headline. You can attract more readers while simplifying your editing job *and* improving the layout by including kickers (a short line above the headline) and decks (further description of the article below the headline) along with the headlines of longer articles.

Use kickers to classify articles and get reader attention. A kicker is a good place for a *label head* or *standing head*. It will alert the intended reader to the general subject of the article (committee notes, maintenance report, union summary, attention flight attendants). Kickers don't need action verbs.

Use decks to tell more of the story and lead the reader into the lead paragraph. Both kickers and decks help enhance the look of the page.

STOCK UPDATE

Falling bond prices good news for stockholders

Prices soar to highest value in history, President Bob Ulrich tells why

---

You learn much more at a glance with the kicker and deck than you would if the article were simply titled, "Stock Update."

Creating Digestible Bites With Subheads

Use subheads to break the text of long articles into unintimidating sections. About every three to five paragraphs, write a mini-headline following the rules for writing good headlines. Summarize the contents of the section for readers. Set the subheads in bold type.

Sometimes, space is so tight that you don't have room for subheads. Another technique is to put the first two or three words in boldface or capital letters every few paragraphs.

quis nostrud esta exerci tation ullamcorper suscipit laboris nisl ut aliquip ex ea commodo con sequat. Duis autem vel eum irure dolor in henderit in vulputate velit esse consequat.

How to get paid on time
Vel illum dolor eu feugiat mulla facilsi at vero eos et accusm et ius to omnis voluptas assumenda est, mnis repellend.

Keeps payables current
Temporibud auteui quinsud et aur offik debit aut tum rerum necessit atib saepe evenit ut er mosit non recusand. Itaque earun rerum hic ten tury sapiente delectus au aut perfer zim edndis dolorib asperiore repellat.

Subheads encourage your readers to keep reading.

Ut wise enim ad minim veniam, quis nostrud esta exerci tation ullamcorper suscipit laboris nisl ut aliquip ex ea commodo con sequat. Duis autem vel eum irure dolor in henderit in vulputate velit esse consequat.

Getting paid on time is one of the software's best benefits. Vel illum dolor eu feugiat mulla facilsi at vero eos et accusm et ius to odio dignessim qui blandt prae sent possum omnis voluptas assumenda est, mnis repellend.

By keeping your payables current, the system pays for itself in a matter of months. Temporibud auteui quinsud et aur offik debit aut tum rerum necessit atib saepe evenit ut er mosit non recusand. Itaque earun rerum hic ten tury sapiente delectus au aut perfer zim edndis dolorib asperiore repellat. Hanc ego cum teme senteniam, quid est kur

If you don't have room for subheads, setting the first few words in boldface is a good alternative.

CAPTIVATING CAPTIONS

Capture more readers and lead them into your articles by giving special attention to *captions* or *cutlines* (i.e., the text that accompanies and describes the significance of a photo or illustration). When readers first glance at a page, their eyes go to photographs or illustrations. They next move to the caption. Include a caption with every illustration in your layout. Write it in a way that will make readers want to read the article.

Here are a few rules for writing captions.

1. Be sure it identifies all people shown and that it does not announce what is obvious: *"This is a cow." "Shown here receiving..."*
2. Stress the story behind the photo. With a simple mug shot, add a quote or a teaser line: *Moses Campbell ... a winning idea.*
3. Add and explain significant facts that can't be ascertained from the photograph.
4. If a sign is shown in a foreign language, translate the sign message in the cutline.

Captions can be enhanced by the use of a small kicker above the caption, or by putting the first couple of words of the caption in heavier type such as boldface or boldface caps.

NEW FACES:
Sam Smith brings 15 years of sales experience to Acme Printing Company.

In addition to their use with headlines, kickers can also accompany captions.

PRINCIPLES OF PULL QUOTES

In addition to the standard text found in most publications, you can create other words that work as visuals in the layout. An effective use of type as a design tool is the pull quote (i.e., the print equivalent of the sound bite). Pull quotes work well in newsletters with long articles and few graphics.

Extract dramatic quotes or statements from stories; set them in a different typeface, and run them boxed in the text. This breaks up large areas of gray and induces the reader to read a story.

The best rules for writing pull quotes we've come across are from publication design trainer Polly Pattison. Her "Pattison's Principles for Pull Quotes" are: 1) include only one theme, 2) keep the length five lines or under and 3) make them quick, visual bites.

Lorem ipsum dolor sit amet, con secteteur adipsicing elit, sed diam nonnumy nibh euisnod tempor inci dunt ut labore et dolore magna ali quam erat volupat.

> **" It was the hardest decision I have ever made... "**

Beating all odds

Ut wise enim ad minim veniam, quis nostrud esta exerci tation ullamcorper suscipit laboris nisl ut aliquip ex ea commodo con sequat. Duis autem vel eum irure dolor in henderit in vulputate velit esse consequat. Vel illum dolor eu feugiat mulla facilsi at

vero eos et accusm et ius to odio dignessim qui blandt prae sent luptatum zzril delenit aigue duos dolore et mosestias exceptur sint occaecat cupidtat not simil pro vident tempor sunt in culpa qui officia desrunt mollit aniom ib est abor un et dolor fuga.

Et harumd dereud facilis est er expedit distint. Nam liber tempor cum soluta nobis eligent option congue nibil impediet doming id quod maxim plecat facer possum omnis voluptas assumenda est, mnis repellend.

Temporibud auteui quinsud et aur offik debit aut tum rerum necessit atib saepe evenit ut er mosit non recusand. Itaque earun rerum hic ten tury sapiente delectus au aut perfer zim edndis dolorib asperiore repellat. Hanc ego cum teme senteniam.

If your page is void of visuals, consider sprucing it up with a pull quote. Choose a quote to intrigue readers

PULLING IN READERS WITH TEASERS

Aside from pull quotes, other ways to "tease" readers into the newsletter are contents boxes (i.e., a table of contents detailing stories on inside pages, set in a box on the front page), teasers on the mailing panel (words promoting the stories in the newsletter set near the mailing address) and other small announcements within the newsletter.

Put on your marketing hat when you write teasers. Think of the "hooks" that attract readers. When writing table of contents text, list the headline of the article (or a shortened version) and a line below describing further why readers should turn to the article. List page numbers along with the teaser text.

Box off teasers, place them in the margins surrounded by white space or use the blank space near the mailing address.

Every publication has busy readers. Encourage people to spend time with you by "selling" your newsletter content with teasers.

Read On ☞

☞ New health care benefits start next week
see page 2

☞ How to earn more from the stock option plan
see page 3

☞ Earn back to school tuition dollars
see page 3

☞ Competitiveness training program to start soon
see page 4

Chapter 9

Reader-Friendly Designs

*Setting words into type requires
a knowledge of what makes type legible
and what makes it readable.*

READABILITY & THE RIGHT "LOOK"

In the days before desktop computers, most newsletters were either typed or typeset. Typed newsletters had limited choices of design—usually one column, one or two typefaces. The editors of typeset newsletters were often helped by professional designers.

Today, most editors design and lay out their own newsletters using desktop publishing systems. Your job is to present the news you have so carefully gathered and written. The paper the newsletter is printed on, the typefaces it is written in and the size and spacing of this type are part of the design. They all must be carefully chosen both for readability and for the right "look."

This chapter covers ways to make your words look good in print. It concentrates on the design of the words, when in reality, good designs are created by effective combinations of words and graphics. (To learn more about publication design, see Appendix 5 for a listing of further resources.)

Setting your words into type requires a knowledge of what makes type *legible*—how each letter looks on the page—as well as what makes it *readable*—how easy it is to read and comprehend sentences, paragraphs and articles.

SELECTING PAPER & SIZES

To assure optimum legibility of type, choose a light paper color such as white or cream. Dark papers can turn words into mush. Choose a paper of medium weight (60 or 70 pound text), one that will not allow the ink to bleed through and show up on the other side of the page. This is often the case when newsprint is printed on two sides.

Reading comprehension studies show that the finish of the paper—glossy, matte or uncoated—does not affect the ease of reading of the type on the page. (When light reflects off of glossy paper, readers simply adjust the angle of the page.)

Paper choice also depends on other considerations such as the need for flexibility and the image you want to convey to readers.

Heavy, glossy paper presents a more affluent image than light-weight uncoated or newsprint stock. Consider recycled paper and soy-based ink if you want to present an environmentally conscious image. (Since many recycled papers don't look like they're recycled, include the recycling logo in your masthead.)

Many newsletters are printed on 11x17-inch paper and folded to create letter-sized pages. This is a good format because it is simple to handle, economical and easy to set up on desktop publishing systems, many of which use a letter-sized page as the default page size.

If the amount of news available for an issue increases, you can easily insert an extra 8 1/2x11-inch sheet into this format.

You may want to stay with an old-fashioned "news letter" form, stapling together as many 8 1/2x11-inch sheets as required for each issue. This is the size of many newsletters reproduced on office equipment (though more expensive copiers can handle 11x17-sized sheets).

Explore the possibilities of various paper sizes and weights, and talk to a printer about the best paper for the best price.

FINDING LEGIBLE TYPEFACES

There are literally thousands of typefaces available for most desktop and word processing systems. Single-subject newsletters such as Kiplinger's and other brief financial letters, as well as any true letter-style newsletter, may be printed in one typeface. This appropriately gives a sense of immediacy to the news.

But in most newsletters that bring private news and announcements to a specific audience every few weeks, one typeface can get boring.

For variety, use two or three legible faces. Use one typeface for the body copy. News headlines can be set in the same typeface as the body copy or can take another typeface. Standing heads can be set in another typeface—the same type used in the nameplate works well—or you can use the headline or body copy face.

Some of the best typefaces available are those from the Adobe Type Collection. See Appendix 5 for more information on these typefaces and the illustration below for some examples.

This is Bauer Bodoni	This is Garamond
This is Century Old Style	This is Goudy
This is Cheltenham	This is Palatino
This is Galliard	This is Times Roman

These sample typefaces work well for newsletter body copy.

This is Eras

This is Futura

This is Helvetica

This is Stone Sans

These typefaces work well for headlines.

Futura in Headlines

This Bauer Bodoni works well for body copy. This Bauer Bodoni works well for body copy. This Bauer Bodoni works well for body copy. This Bauer Bodoni works well for body copy. This Bauer Bodoni works well for body copy. This Bauer Bodoni works well for body copy.

Eras Works Too

This Garamond creates light and friendly body copy. This Garamond creates light and friendly body copy. This Garamond creates light and friendly body copy. This Garamond creates light and friendly body copy. This Garamond creates light and friendly body copy. This Garamond creates light and friendly body copy.

Good newsletter headline typefaces stand out on the page. They look "black" on the page when you hold it at a distance. Good body copy faces are easy to read and create a light gray on the page.

MATCHING TYPE SIZES TO AUDIENCE

Readability studies have shown that at different ages, people prefer different type sizes. Let the age of your audience determine the type sizes you choose.

Type sizes are stated in units of measurement called points.

1 point   = $^1/_{72}$ inch
12 points   =   1 pica
6 picas   =   1 inch

If most of your readers are 65 and over, select a large type size. Large-print books for older persons and persons with certain visual limitations are set in 14-point and 18-point type. Even many legally "blind" people can read very large type such as 18-point type.

But for most general readership newsletters, 10- or 11-point typefaces will be appropriate. Set headlines in sizes between 14 and 30 points on a standard 8½x11-inch page. Anything larger will look odd; anything smaller will be too nearly the size of the body text to achieve proper headline emphasis.

This 14-point type is used for people with visual limitations as well as for beginning readers.

This 12-point type is good for older readers.

This 11-point type is a good text size for newsletters.

This 10.5-point type can be created in some layout programs.

This 10-point type is also a good text size for newsletters.

Select type sizes based on the average age of your readers. Note that your desktop publishing system may allow you to create point sizes in .1 increments—making possible a compromise in type size such as the 10.5 point shown above.

EMPHASIZING WITH TYPE STYLES

Within a given typeface, several type styles are almost always available: roman (regular), *italic*, **bold**, and ***bold italic***.

Roman describes the general family of typefaces used in the text of almost everything you read, including what you're reading now. Roman denotes that letters are straight up and down; that is, the vertical lines of the letters form a right angle to the horizontal line of the page. There are hundreds of different designs of roman type. This book is set in one called Goudy Old Style.

Italic type slants to the right. It is generally used to emphasize words and passages, and often used in figure legends, captions and cutlines, i.e., the copy that accompanies and describes a photograph or a technical illustration.

Bold type is also useful for **emphasizing short passages in the text.** Bold is preferred over underlining because the <u>underline style in desktop publishing software cuts through letters such as y and p</u>.

SELECTING A TYPEFACE FOR BODY COPY

All typefaces are either *serif* or *sans serif*. The letters in a serif typeface have small extra strokes at the ends of the lines that form the letters. Goudy Old Style is a serif typeface. Within serif faces, the *old styles* have slanted serifs; *modern* faces have straight serifs (see illustration below).

The first "f" is Goudy Old Style. The second is a modern face, Bodoni.

This is Helvetica. It is a sans serif typeface.

This is Galliard. It is a serif typeface.

Helvetica gives text a different "feel" than Galliard.

Now look closely at Helvetica, a sans serif typeface illustrated above. You will see that every letter in it is made of an unadorned straight or curved line. Many people dote on sans serif typefaces, regarding them as elegant, spare and clean, which they are. There is no controversy about their usefulness in headlines and other short lines of type. They are ideal for such uses. But there is great controversy about their use in long passages of type. Sans serif faces should *not* be used for full-length news or feature stories.

Many readability studies support the opinion that serif typefaces are easier to read. When one newspaper, the old *New York World Journal Tribune*, switched from a sans serif to a serif typeface, its circulation increased. So did the morale of its staff.

It is thought that the reason for the better readability of serif typefaces is that the serifs give readers added clues to quickly distinguish letters. The letters—and words—do not all look so much alike. If you use a sans serif type for sections of the body copy, shorten the line length.

One other factor to remember is that one typeface will appear larger than another typeface of the same point size. Type is measured from the top of *ascenders* on letters such as *d, l* and *k* to the bottom of *descenders* on letters such as *j, y, p* and *g*. An *ascender* is the part of a letter that extends above the body of the letter; a *descender* is the part that extends below it. Short letters, like the lower-case *x*, have neither ascenders nor descenders. Typefaces with short ascenders and descenders have a larger *x-height*, i.e., the height of the lower case *x*. The larger the x-height, the larger the typeface looks on the page.

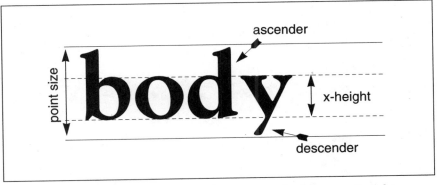

The ascender, descender and x-height play a part in the "character" of the typeface.

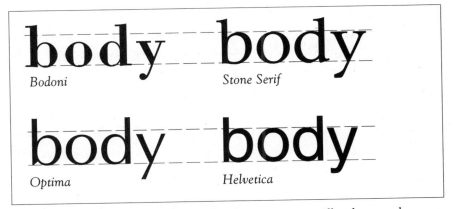

The x-height of a typeface will cause it to look larger or smaller than another. Bodoni looks smaller than Stone Serif and Optima looks smaller than Helvetica. All are set in the same size.

Choose typefaces and sizes that will not distract the reader from the news content. Avoid typefaces that are too bold and fat or too light and thin. Avoid ones that are too condensed or extended. Avoid all elaborate typefaces for use in news text copy. For example, script type is intended to imitate handwriting and is therefore used only when you wish to convey intimacy. Use it in announcements and invitations. Do not use it for news stories.

This is Avant Garde
This is Bookman
This is Tiffany

These typefaces take up too much space in newsletter body copy or headlines.

This is Helvetica Compressed
This is Futura Condensed

This typefaces are too narrow for newsletter body copy but can be used for tall, attractive headlines.

If, when you are looking through a typeface book, a typeface catches your eye—and you find yourself saying something like, "Oh, isn't that interesting!"—don't choose that typeface for news text. It may, however, be all right for some headlines.

Choose clear, readable roman typefaces for text, ones that convey a sensible, professional image and that are the right size for your readers. Choose headline typefaces that emphasize the text and enhance the page.

ESTABLISHING HEADLINE TYPEFACES & SIZES

For headline type, use faces that harmonize with the text face. While serif type is best for text, both serif and sans serif typefaces work well in headlines. Some complementary typefaces, such as Stone Serif and Stone Sans Serif, are designed to work together. One way to assure type harmony is to choose body copy and headline typefaces that have roughly the same x-height. This makes combinations like Helvetica and Times (caution: people are pretty sick of this one), Eras and Garamond, and Franklin Gothic and Palatino work.

In addition to selecting the headline typeface, decide the standard sizes and styles you'll use in each issue. Headline size and style identify the news value and character of the story. Limit the number of sizes to three or four, and use them consistently to signal what the reader will find beneath them:

1. *Large bold headlines for important news stories.* These headlines run across the top of an entire page, or two-thirds of it or half of it, depending on how big you want your biggest headlines to be.

2. *Secondary headlines for lesser news stories.* These are smaller and/or lighter than the number-one headlines. They go with stories of secondary importance, usually shorter than the major stories.

3. *Heads for features and editorials.* These variety headlines go with features or items that are not straight news. They may be used with rules or boxes for emphasis and design interest on a page layout.

4. *Heads for short news items.* These headlines usually run one column wide on short news stories (brief summaries containing roughly three paragraphs).

The size of headlines signals to readers the importance of each article.

Limitation of size and style is important unless you want to project a jumbled look—which probably you do not. Select your headline styles carefully.

Experiment with different typefaces and type styles. Try boldface and italic. Try the same headline written in different patterns on the page. Write it all on one line; then try the same headline written on two or three lines. Try different widths, across one, two or three columns.

Try some headlines with a *kicker*, a line written in smaller, lighter type than the main headline and run above it. The smaller line might be in *italic*. Try a *hammerhead*, in which the top line is in larger type and the second line is in the smaller. Try a *deck* headline, one with two or three smaller, lighter lines of type under two or three lines in larger, bolder type.

PageMaker used most often for newsletters
but QuarkXPress Windows version gains ground quickly

A hammerhead has larger type on the top line and smaller type on the bottom.

Working with published examples will give you a proper feel for headline types and uses. Study those used in newspapers and magazines, how they look and when and where they are used.

Notice that very few headlines are set in all capital letters. Numerous studies have shown that capital-lettered headlines slow down reading. (If you do use all capital headlines or subheads, use the small caps feature as is done in the subheads of this book.) Many headline writers capitalize the first letter of each word except for prepositions and articles, to emphasize key news words. But the trend now is to use the same capitalization rules in headlines that are used in writing sentences.

Develop a schedule that suits your newsletter style and subject matter. List it in your stylebook.

Garamond 30-pt bold

1. **Heads for important news items** are 30-point Garamond bold. They run across two or three columns and are flush left.

Futura 14-pt bold

Kickers for main news items are 14-point Futura bold. Kickers should not run more than halfway across the head and are set flush left.

Garamond 18-pt italic

Decks used on important stories are 18-point Garamond italic. Decks run the full length of the headline and are set flush left.

Garamond 24-pt bold

2. **Heads for secondary news items** are 24-point Garamond bold. They are run across one or two columns.

Futura 12-pt bold

Kickers for secondary news items are 12-point Futura bold. Kickers should not run more than halfway across the head.

Futura 16-pt bold

3. **Heads for sidebars** and other specialty items are 16-point Futura bold. They run across one or two columns.

Garamond 14-pt bold

4. **Heads for newsbriefs** are 14-point Garamond bold. They run across one column.

Make a list of your headline sizes and styles along with the usage for each.

The way the type ends up looking on the page depends largely on the number of columns on the page (or page *grid*). And the page grid is often limited by the capabilities of the publishing software. Most newsletter publishers either use word processing or desktop publishing software.

THE WORD PROCESSED NEWSLETTER

Simply designed newsletters tend to get apologized for. "It is not much to look at," the editor says, "we just do it with our old word processing software." And, for sure, some newsletters are nothing to brag about—the ones typed in single spaced lines completely across each page. Such a solid "gray" page is uninviting.

But some very appealing publications are typewritten or word processed. The famous Kiplinger newsletter is typewritten—or it *looks* like it is. The handsome word processed publication, like the handsome desktop published conforms to basic principles of design(see example on next page).

One distinct advantage of the typewritten newsletter is that it looks timely and personal. If it is a daily, with content so timely that any delay in reaching readers will render the news valueless, then simple word processing is probably preferable to a fancy layout.

THE DESKTOP PUBLISHED NEWSLETTER

Desktop publishing software offers the possibility of attractive, multi-column, well-designed newsletters. We use the word "possibility" because simple ownership of the right software doesn't mean that the operator can produce such a layout. Some desktop publishing programs still create awkward word spacing and hyphenation. The ease of reversing type, changing type sizes and underlining text may encourage you to stray from accepted design principles.

Desktop published newsletters usually use either one, two or three columns. Some are up to four columns. If you choose a four-column layout, use a smaller type size or there will be too many gaps between

Template ideas for publishers   **January 1996**

Strong, bold, somewhat long headline

Lorem ipsum dolor sit amet, con secteteur adipsicing elit, sed diam nonnumy nibh euisnod tempor inci dunt ut labore et dolore magna ali quam erat volupat. Ut wise enim ad minim veniam, quis nostrud exerci tation ullamcorper suscipit laboris nisl ut aliquip ex ea commodo con sequat. Duis autem vel eum irure dolor in henderit in vulputate velit esse consequat.

Vel illum dolor eu feugiat mulla facilsi at vero eos et accusm et ius to odio dignessim qui blandt prae sent luptatum zzril delenit aigue duos dolore et mosestias exceptur sint occaecat cupidtat not simil pro vident tempor sunt in culpa qui officia desrunt mollit aniom ib est abor un.

When using a one-column template

Lorem ipsum dolor sit amet, con secteteur adipsicing elit, sed diam nonnumy nibh euisnod tempor inci dunt ut labore et dolore magna ali quam erat volupat. Ut wise enim ad minim veniam, quis nostrud exerci tation ullamcorper suscipit laboris nisl ut aliquip ex ea commodo con sequat. Duis autem vel eum irure dolor in henderit in vulputate velit esse consequat.

Vel illum dolor eu feugiat mulla facilsi at vero eos et accusm et ius to odio dignessim qui blandt prae sent luptatum zzril delenit aigue duos dolore et mosestias exceptur sint occaecat cupidtat not simil pro vident tempor sunt in culpa qui officia desrunt mollit aniom ib est abor un.

Large body copy & plenty of white space

Lorem ipsum dolor sit amet, con secteteur adipsicing elit, sed diam nonnumy nibh euisnod tempor inci dunt ut labore et dolore magna ali quam erat volupat. Ut wise enim ad minim veniam, quis nostrud exerci tation ullamcorper suscipit laboris nisl ut aliquip ex ea commodo con sequat. Duis autem vel eum irure dolor in henderit in vulputate velit esse consequat.

Vel illum dolor eu feugiat mulla facilsi at vero eos et accusm et ius to odio dignessim qui blandt prae sent luptatum zzril delenit aigue duos dolore et mosestias exceptur sint occaecat cupidtat not simil pro vident.

Simple layouts with strategic use of white space keeps all-text newsletters inviting. The narrow left hand column containing the headlines is called a scholar's margin. Use of a scholar's margin adds white space to the layout and keeps the text from looking too long.

words and too many hyphenated words. (Depending on the age of your target audience, a small type size may be inappropriate, eliminating the option of a four-column design.)

Template ideas for publishers   **January 1996**

Try "snaking" headlines

Lorem ipsum dolor sit amet, con secteteur adipsicing elit, sed diam nonnumy nibh euisnod tempor inci dunt ut labore et dolore magna ali quam erat volupat. Ut wise enim ad minim veniam, quis nostrud exerci tation ullamcorper suscipit laboris nisl ut aliquip ex ea commodo con sequat. Duis autem vel eum irure dolor in henderit in vulputate velit esse consequat.

Vel illum dolor eu feugiat mulla facilsi at vero eos et accusm et ius to odio dignessim qui blandt prae sent luptatum zzril delenit aigue duos dolore et mosestias exceptur sint occaecat cupidtat not simil pro vident tempor sunt in culpa qui officia desrunt mollit aniom ib est abor un.

Vel illum dolor eu feugiat mulla facilsi at vero eos et accusm et ius to odio dignessim qui blandt prae sent luptatum zzril delenit aigue duos dolore et mosestias exceptur sint occaecat cupidtat not simil pro vident tempor sunt in culpa qui officia desrunt mollit aniom ib est abor un.

Eliminating "tombstones"

Lorem ipsum dolor sit amet, con secteteur adipsicing elit, sed diam nonnumy nibh euisnod tempor inci dunt ut labore et dolore magna ali quam erat volupat. Ut wise enim ad minim veniam, quis nostrud exerci tation ullamcorper suscipit laboris nisl ut aliquip ex ea commodo con sequat. Duis autem vel eum irure dolor in henderit in vulputate velit esse consequat.

Vel illum dolor eu feugiat mulla facilsi at vero eos et accusm et ius to odio dignessim qui blandt prae sent luptatum zzril delenit aigue duos dolore et

mosestias exceptur sint occaecat cupidtat not simil pro vident tempor sunt in culpa qui officia desrunt mollit aniom ib est abor un.

Lorem ipsum dolor sit amet, con secteteur adipsicing elit, sed diam nonnumy nibh euisnod tempor inci dunt ut labore et dolore magna ali quam erat volupat. Ut wise enim ad minim veniam, quis nostrud exerci tation ullamcorper suscipit laboris nisl ut aliquip ex ea commodo con sequat. Duis autem vel eum irure dolor in henderit in vulputate velit esse consequat.

Two-column layouts can get pretty boring

Lorem ipsum dolor sit amet, con secteteur adipsicing elit, sed diam nonnumy nibh euisnod tempor inci dunt ut labore et dolore magna ali quam erat volupat. Ut wise enim ad minim veniam, quis nostrud exerci tation ullamcorper suscipit laboris nisl ut aliquip ex ea commodo con sequat. Duis autem vel eum irure dolor in henderit in vulputate velit esse consequat.

Vel illum dolor eu feugiat mulla facilsi at vero eos et accusm et ius to odio dignessim qui blandt prae sent luptatum zzril delenit aigue duos dolore et mosestias exceptur sint occaecat cupidtat not simil pro vident.

Lorem ipsum dolor sit amet, con secteteur adipsicing elit, sed diam nonnumy nibh euisnod tempor inci dunt ut labore et dolore magna ali quam erat volupat. Ut wise enim ad minim veniam, quis nostrud exerci tation ullamcorper suscipit laboris nisl ut aliquip ex ea commodo con sequat. Duis autem vel eum irure dolor in henderit in vulputate velit esse consequat.

Two-column designs work well for text-only newsletters or when using only one or two graphics. When photographs and illustrations are used regularly, consider a three-column design.

The most common grid for newsletters is three columns. This provides an opportunity for a variety in page layout and photo sizes. Regardless of the grid you choose, strive for a readable page.

TEMPLATE TRENDS

Template ideas for publishers   **January 1996**

3-column with lead story on left

Lorem ipsum dolor sit amet, con secteteur adipsicing elit, sed diam nonnumy nibh euisnod tempor inci dunt ut labore et dolore magna ali quam erat volupat. Ut wise enim ad minim veniam, quis nostrud exerci tation ullamcorper suscipit laboris nisl ut aliquip ex ea commodo con sequat. Duis autem vel eum irure dolor in henderit in vulputate velit esse consequat.

Vel illum dolor eu feugiat mulla facilsi at vero eos et accusm et ius to odio dignessim qui blandt prae sent luptatum zzril delenit aigue duos dolore et mosestias exceptur sint occaecat cupidtat not simil pro vident

tempor sunt in culpa qui officia desrunt mollit aniom ib est abor un.

Vel illum dolor eu feugiat mulla facilsi at vero eos et accusm et ius to odio dignessim qui blandt prae sent luptatum zzril delenit aigue duos dolore et mosestias exceptur sint occaecat cupidtat not simil pro vident tempor sunt in culpa qui officia desrunt mollit aniom ib est abor un.

Vel illum dolor eu feugiat mulla facilsi at vero eos et accusm et ius to odio dignessim qui blandt prae sent luptatum zzril delenit aigue duos dolore et mosestias exceptur sint occaecat cupidtat not simil pro vident tempor sunt in culpa qui.

Vel illum dolor eu feugiat mulla facilsi at vero eos et accusm et ius.

Good spot for lists, boxes or graphics

1. Lorem ipsum dolor sit amet, con secteteur adipsicing elit, sed diam nonnumy nibh.

2. Lorem ipsum dolor sit amet, con secteteur adipsicing elit, sed diam nonnumy nibh.

3. Lorem ipsum dolor sit amet, con secteteur adipsicing elit, sed diam nonnumy nibh.

4. Lorem ipsum dolor sit amet, con secteteur adipsicing elit, sed diam nonnumy nibh.

5. Lorem ipsum dolor sit amet, con secteteur adipsicing elit, sed diam nonnumy nibh.

A second story follows here

Lorem ipsum dolor sit amet, con secteteur adipsicing elit, sed diam nonnumy nibh euisnod tempor inci dunt ut labore et dolore magna ali quam erat volupat. Ut wise enim ad minim veniam, quis nostrud exerci tation ullamcorper suscipit laboris nisl ut aliquip ex ea commodo con sequat. Duis autem vel eum irure dolor in henderit in vulputate velit esse consequat.

Vel illum dolor eu feugiat mulla facilsi at vero eos et accusm et ius to odio dignessim qui blandt prae sent luptatum zzril delenit aigue duos

dolore et mosestias exceptur sint occaecat cupidtat not simil pro vident tempor sunt in culpa qui officia desrunt mollit aniom ib est abor un.

Lorem ipsum dolor sit amet, con secteteur adipsicing elit, sed diam nonnumy nibh euisnod tempor inci dunt ut labore et dolore magna ali quam erat volupat. Ut wise enim ad minim veniam, quis nostrud exerci tation ullamcorper suscipit laboris nisl ut aliquip ex ea commodo con sequat. Duis autem vel eum irure dolor in henderit in vulputate velit esse consequat.

The three-column design is most commonly used for newsletters. It's attractive, flexible and functional for photographs, long features and short news items.

FINDING THE IDEAL LINE LENGTH

The length of each line of type will heavily influence how easy your newsletter is to read. Line length is determined by several of the design choices you make: the typeface you choose and the size you set it in; the number of columns; the page margins and the space between columns.

Two helpful rules will help you when verifying that your line length is reader-friendly. These are the alphabet-and-a-half rule and the points-times-two rule.

Alphabet-and-a-Half. This rule says that a good line length for body copy is roughly 39 characters. Thats 26 plus 13, or the number of letters in the alphabet plus half this number.

Points-Times-Two. After numerous reading comprehension studies at the University of Maryland, Edmund Arnold determined that the ideal line length (in picas) is found by taking the type size and multiplying it by two. This gives 11-point type an ideal line length of 22 picas (3.66 inches).

> This is the line length resulting from 10-point Times Roman type set on a three-column design with four-pica (.66-inch) margins and one pica (.167 inch) between columns. The line length is 12 picas (2 inches). The number of characters per line is 39.

This is an ideal line length according to the alphabet-and-a-half rule.

> This is the line length resulting from 10-point Times Roman type set on a two-column design with five-pica (.83-inch) margins and one pica (.167 inch) between columns. The line length is 20 picas (3.33 inches). The number of characters per line is 59.

This is an ideal length following the points-times-two rule. Use these two rules to give yourself a range to stay within.

PLUNGING INTO PICAS

Most newsletter editors do not have the benefit of formal design training. As such, the unit of measurement we're most comfortable with is inches. The default settings in our desktop publishing software are in inches, and paper sizes are measured this way too.

But picas have their place in publication design. Newsletter layouts involve small pieces that are difficult to measure in inches. Often pages need to be segmented into thirds (to create a letter fold, for example). Dividing an 11-inch long page into thirds makes each section 3.66 inches long. It is difficult to find this spot on your page ruler. But in picas, a letter-sized page breaks into even segments of 22 picas.

Ruler in Inches:

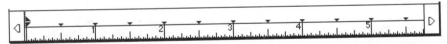

Ruler in Picas:

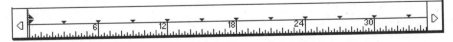

Though the default measurement system in most publishing programs is inches, most professional designers work in picas.

Picas also have a more direct relationship to points, the measurement system used to measure type. Twelve points equal one pica, rather than taking 72 points to reach one inch.

The easiest way to take the plunge into picas is to change the measurement default in your desktop publishing software (this is under "preferences" in most programs). In PageMaker, for example, you'll see that this changes the default setting of space between columns to an even one pica instead of .167 inches. But don't stop here. More defaults await your watchful eye.

WHEN TO CHANGE DEFAULT SETTINGS

While your desktop publishing system makes producing your newsletter easier, you need to be aware of certain pre-set settings (called defaults) that you may want to override.

Leading. The space between each line of type is called leading (rhymes with *wedding*). The "auto" setting in most programs is the point size plus two points. For example, the default setting for 10-point type is 12-point leading. For column lengths such as those shown on page 128, you can reduce the leading to 11 or 11.5 point.

The auto setting, or slightly larger, is good for very long or very short lines of type. For example, a 12-point leading is comfortable when setting 10-point type in a 10-pica column. The extra line space helps the eye keep its place when going from one line to the next. Be careful not to add too much leading or you'll defeat its purpose.

Short lines of type set right on top of one another are hard to read. The eye struggles to bounce from line to line quickly. Add an extra point or two of leading between the lines.

This 10-point Times Roman with 10-point leading is too compact.

Short lines of type set right on top of one another are hard to read. The eye struggles to bounce from line to line quickly. Add an extra point or two of leading between the lines.

This 10-point Times Roman with 16-point leading is too "loose."

Short lines of type set right on top of one another are hard to read. The eye struggles to bounce from line to line quickly. Add an extra point or two of leading between the lines.

This 10-point Times Roman with "auto" or 12-point leading is comfortable to read.

Space Between Columns. A good distance between columns is one pica (.167 inch). This is the default in PageMaker. Other popular programs such as WordPerfect use 1.5 picas (.25 inches) as a default. This is too wide for most page layouts.

If you must set columns closer than one pica, use a hairline rule to separate columns.

Columns should be separated vertically by at least 12 points (one pica). If they are set closer together than that, a hairline rule should separate columns. Columns should be separated vertically by at least 12 points.

Columns should be separated vertically by at least 12 points (one pica). If they are set closer together than that, a hairline rule should separate columns. Columns should be separated vertically by at least 12 points.

A comfortable distance between two columns is one pica (.167 inch).

Columns should be separated vertically by at least 12 points (one pica). If they are set closer together than that, a hairline rule should separate columns. Columns should be separated vertically by at least 12 points.

Columns should be separated vertically by at least 12 points (one pica). If they are set closer together than that, a hairline rule should separate columns. Columns should be separated vertically by at least 12 points.

One-and-a-half picas (.25 inches) is usually too large of a space.

Columns should be separated vertically by at least 12 points (one pica). If they are set closer together than that, a hairline rule should separate columns. Columns should be separated vertically by at least 12 points.

Columns should be separated vertically by at least 12 points (one pica). If they are set closer together than that, a hairline rule should separate columns. Columns should be separated vertically by at least 12 points.

If using less than one pica, (.75 pica shown here), run a hairline rule between columns.

Justified vs. Unjustfied. Another decision in setting up columns is whether to set the type with *justified* or *unjustified* margins. A justified margin is one in which every line ends at the same place. Thus, you can lay a ruler along the right edge of a column of justified type, and each line will meet it. An unjustified or *ragged right* margin means that some lines will be a few units shorter than others. Most programs are set up with unjustified as the default.

There is a trend toward the use of the ragged right margin, because it is freer, more natural, and less formal than the justified margin. Some studies suggest that it is more readable while others say that justified is best for reading comprehension.

Since the jury is out on this issue, check the capabilities of your software. If justifying columns both right and left creates gaping spaces between words, these gaps are ugly to the eye and can distract the reader from story content. You're better off running columns ragged right.

This is a justified margin. A justified margin is one in which every line ends at the same place. Thus, you can lay a ruler along the right edge of this column and each line meets it.

This is an unjustified margin. Some lines are shorter than others. This is an unjustified margin. Some lines are shorter than others. This is an unjustified margin. Some lines are shorter than others.

Justified margins are even on both sides (top paragraph). Unjustified margins are ragged to the right (bottom paragraph).

Hyphenation Zone. If you use a ragged right margin, note that most desktop publishing software can control what's called the "hyphenation zone." Setting a smaller hyphenation zone avoids a too ragged right margin.

If you use a ragged right margin, note that most desktop publishing software can control what's called the "hyphenation zone." Setting a smaller hyphenation zone avoids too ragged of a right margin. If you use a ragged right margin, note that most desktop publishing software can control what's called the "hyphenation zone."	If you use a ragged right margin, note that most desktop publishing software can control what's called the "hyphenation zone." Setting a smaller hyphenation zone avoids too ragged of a right margin. If you use a ragged right margin, note that most desktop publishing software can control what's called the "hyphenation zone."

Note the difference in the hyphenation zones of the two paragraphs. The first has a four-pica zone and is much more ragged than the one-pica zone of the second.

Indents & Tabs. The default indent in most word processing programs is three picas (.5 inches). This indent is too deep for most newsletter text. Depending on the size of your type, set indents to between one and two picas (.167 to .333 inches— an even .25 inches keeps it simple for those unready for the "pica plunge"). The first paragraph after a headline or subhead doesn't have to be indented.

If you include numbered or bulleted lists in your text, reset the tabs so that when type wraps around for multi-line items, it returns under the other lines of type, not the number or bullet.

Do this...

✓ Pack suitcase and
   cosmetic kit

✓ Turn down furnace
   and shut off water to
   water heater

...not this.

✓   Pack suitcase
and cosmetic kit

✓   Turn down
furnace and shut off
water to water heater

Tracking. One last setting that can greatly improve or impair the readability of your type is the letter and word spacing. Some programs have a feature called "tracking" that adjusts both letter and word spacing to help you increase or decrease the area the type takes in the layout. Many editors use this feature to make copy fit. Others adjust the size or leading of the type (another design no-no).

While you may be filled with glee that your columns end in a perfect line, be aware that tracking that is too loose or too tight makes type harder to read. Instead, learn alternative methods for copyfitting.

One last setting that can greatly improve or impair the readability of your type is the letter and word spacing.

"Very tight" tracking.

One last setting that can greatly improve or impair the readability of your type is the letter and word spacing.

"Tight" tracking.

One last setting that can greatly improve or impair the readability of your type is the letter and word spacing.

"Normal" tracking.

One last setting that can greatly improve or impair the readability of your type is the letter and word spacing.

"Loose" tracking.

One last setting that can greatly improve or impair the readability of your type is the letter and word spacing.

"Very loose" tracking.

COPYFITTING IN THE ELECTRONIC AGE

The typefaces, number of columns and justification system you choose determine the length of articles and headlines that will fit on each page of your layout. If you're a newcomer to news editing, you probably haven't even thought about the notion that headlines and body copy must fit a space, rather than vice versa, but they must.

Both word processing and desktop publishing software allow you to write newsletter articles as you're laying out the newsletter. Don't do it. The do-it-all editor must wear three distinct hats—writer, editor and, lastly, designer. Jumble these roles and you'll jumble your newsletter. Most sophisticated electronic publishers keep editorial and design stages separate.

COUNTING WORDS FOR ARTICLES

How much space do you have in the newsletter for layout? Calculate the number of *column inches* by multiplying the length of one column times the number of columns on a page, times the number of pages in the newsletter. Say your newsletter is four pages (two 8½x11 sheets printed on both sides) in a three-column format. Then— allowing for one-inch margins at the top and bottom of each page— you have three 9-inch columns, or 27 column inches per page, and 108 column inches per issue.

Final copy is typeset into the column width you have chosen: about two inches wide in a three-column layout on an 8½x11 page, or three inches wide in a two-column layout on an 8½x11 page. Measure to see how many column inches of written copy you have in these columns.

Remember that everything—all graphics and photos, name-plate, masthead, mailing indicia and space (if the publication is a self-mailer) and headlines must come out of the total column-inch measure. So, by the time you have made space for all of them, and depending on how much white space you use, you may want only about 60 to 80 column inches of written material for a 108-column-inch newsletter. If you have 102 column inches of written copy, plus photos and graphics, something is going to get squeezed: You will have to start editing in earnest: cutting out copy, reducing photos, making headlines shorter. Plan ahead.

Assign word counts. Know how many words fit into a column inch of your newsletter. Count the number of words that standard articles take. Use the word count feature in your word processing program when writing or editing articles.

▤ **Word Count** ▤			
	Main Text	**Footnotes**	**Total**
☒ **Characters**	1055	0	1055
☒ **Words**	156	0	156
☐ **Lines**			
☒ **Paragraphs**	8	0	8

[**Count**] [**Cancel**]

Most word processing software contains a word count feature.

MAKING HEADLINES FIT

No matter how well a headline tells the story, no matter how attractive it is, it must fit the space available for it. The writer who is also the editor and desktop publisher has the apparent advantage of being able to alter layout to fit the headline. But it is better to avoid this temptation: inconsistency and sloppiness of appearance, not to mention the possibility of typographical errors, are a sure result of such a practice.

If a headline is only *slightly* too long for the space, you may "kern the head," that is, squeeze the letters together slightly, or you could reduce the type size a point or two. Some layout programs let you condense or scale the typeface. But, again, too much of this kind of practice will produce erratic pages.

Once you have a model headline schedule, write headlines to fit into one of the styles you have established. To fit headlines, count either words or characters.

When you have used a headline in a newsletter, note the count, enter that information along with the headline into your headline schedule file. Later, when you choose a similar head for a story, you will know how it looks and what the approximate count will be.

Write Headlines That Fit

Write Headlines That Fit

Write Headlines That Fit

The first headline is set with default kerning. The letter spacing of the second headline is squeezed to bring it all onto one line. The third is kerned to give more space between the "rit" in "Write" and the "Fi" in "Fit."

Although it is not necessary that a head completely fill a line, especially when the headline is flush left (i.e., lined up with the left margin), a headline should come close to filling a line. Avoid justifying headlines to both the left and right margins (force justified). Headlines with gaping holes look unprofessional and ragged. Usually the writer could have filled the space with more information (see examples on next page).

Writing headlines

Writing headlines that work

Make full use of the room you have for headlines. Use it to tell readers what they'll gain by reading the article.

AVOIDING 7 DESIGN CULPRITS

Once you fire up your desktop computer, design gremlins dance around you. Design techniques that are, in their own right, attractive and aesthetic are murder on your reader's comprehension. We've already mentioned some do's and don'ts above. Others include:

1. Avoid setting body copy in reverse (white type on a colored background).
2. Watch for excessive, gaping leading.
3. Use black ink for type.
4. Always place the headline *above* the article it introduces.
5. Avoid placing type behind halftone screens heavier than 10 to 20 percent (when using black ink)
6. Don't continue articles to inside pages.
7. Don't place periods at the ends of headlines.

Almost everyone reading this book has violated at least one of these rules and will most likely have trouble agreeing with all of them. But each one is backed up by extensive research from the recently published book, *Type and Layout*, listed in Appendix 5. The author conducted a study of 500 participants and carefully researched the effect on comprehension of each of the common design decisions. (Two previously established rules—one forbidding

large blocks of type in italics, and the other asserting that comprehension of text set in ragged right columns and in fully justified
columns is the same—are thwarted by the research.)

> For most typefaces, a 10 or 20 percent
> screened box will not interfere with the
> legibility of the face. Heavier screens can
> make it hard to read the text. For most
> typefaces, a 10 percent screened box will
> not interfere with the legibility of the face.

> For most typefaces, a 10 or 20 percent
> screened box will not interfere with the
> legibility of the face. Heavier screens can
> make it hard to read the text. For most
> typefaces, a 10 percent screened box will
> not interfere with the legibility of the face.

The 10 percent screen used on the top paragraph shouldn't interfere with reading.
The 30 percent screen (below) is too heavy. Note that a 10 percent screen may
not show up on some desktop outputs. The percentage screen also depends on the
ink color of the screen. A yellow screen can be heavier than a black one.

KICKERS:

Reverse small amounts of type...
it's a kick for any editor

Kickers are an ideal spot to use reverse type.

A light typeface like Goudy Old
Style gets clogged up when set in
reverse. Large amounts of body copy
set this way would be tiring to read
and you'd lose readers. Set only
small amounts of type in reverse.
Use the black and white of reverses
to add another "color" to an otherwise gray page.

Body copy set in reverse is hard to read.

Large amounts of leading give type an inter-

esting look and extra leading has become the

rage among designers. While it's pretty from

a distance, readability suffers. Look out for

your readers and avoid excessive leading.

Large amounts of leading give type an

interesting look and extra leading has become

the rage among designers. While it's pretty

from a distance, readability suffers. Look out

for your readers and avoid excessive leading.

Very wide line spacing is a hot design trend that's not so hot for newsletter readers.

Lorem ipsum dolor sit amet, con secteteur adipsicing elit, sed diam nonnumy nibh euisnod tempor inci dunt ut labore et dolore magna ali quam erat volupat. Ut wise enim ad minim veniam, quis nostrud exerci tation ullamcorper suscipit laboris nisl ut aliquip ex ea commodo con sequat. Duis autem vel eum irure dolor in henderit in vulputate velit esse consequat.

Vel illum dolor eu feugiat mulla facilsi at vero eos et accusm et ius to odio dignessim qui blandt prae sent luptatum zzril delenit aigue duos dolore et mosestias exceptur sint occaecat cupidtat not simil pro vident tempor sunt in culpa qui officia desrunt mollit aniom ib est abor un.

Vel illum dolor eu feugiat mulla facilis at vero eos et accusm et ius to odio dignessim qui blandt prae sent luptatum zzril delenit aigue duos dolore et mosestias exceptur sint occaecat cupidtat not simil pro vident tempor sunt in culpa qui officia desrunt

Readers look below this headline

Lorem ipsum dolor sit amet, con secteteur adipsicing elit, sed diam nonnumy nibh euisnod tempor inci dunt ut labore et dolore magna ali quam erat volupat. Ut wise enim ad minim veniam, quis nostrud exerci tation ullamcorper suscipit laboris nisl ut aliquip ex ea commodo con sequat. Duis autem vel eum irure dolor in henderit in vulputate velit esse consequat.

Vel illum dolor eu feugiat mulla facilsi at vero eos et accusm et ius to odio dignessim qui blandt prae sent luptatum zzril delenit aigue duos

dolore et mosestias exceptur sint occaecat cupidtat not simil pro vident tempor sunt in culpa qui officia desrunt mollit aniom ib est abor un.

Vel illum dolor eu feugiat mulla facilis at vero eos et accusm et ius to odio dignessim qui blandt prae sent luptatum zzril delenit aigue duos dolore et mosestias exceptur sint occaecat cupidtat not simil pro vident tempor sunt in culpa qui officia desrunt mollit aniom ib est abor un.

Vel illum dolor eu feugiat mulla facilis at vero eos et accusm et ius to odio dignessim qui blandt prae sent

Place headlines above the articles they introduce. Though this headline is graphically interesting, readers will start to read below it, rather than at the beginning of the article.

LEARNING BY DOING

While most of us have to learn about design by doing, the benefit of being the editor as well as the designer is that you can protect all of the hard work you've done to collect and write the stories. You want an attractive publication; you also want everyone to read what you've worked so hard to create. As the reader-friendly designer, you'll achieve just that.

Chapter 10

Laying Out Each Issue

What story goes where?
What size should the photos be?
These decisions must be made.

PUTTING IT ALL TOGETHER

When all the elements that make up an issue are gathered, they must be made to fit onto the pages and to do so in proper relation to one another. What story goes where? What size should photos and headlines be with various stories? These are editorial decisions that must be made based on the importance of the news and a keen insight to visual impact.

Preliminary decisions about placement of articles are made by sketching a dummy, i.e., a pattern for the final product. The dummy guides either you or your contracted help when making the layout.

Once the pages are put into rough form, other questions remain. What can be done to break up large, dull areas of nothing but type? This is when a good designer can save you hours of agony.

DUMMYING YOUR LAYOUT

Dummying is making a pattern or sketch for an issue. First make a list of all the stories you have. Rate them by importance. Note those that have photos with them and list other photos that will stand alone. List other material to go into the newsletter—nameplates, mastheads, mailing space, regular columns or standing heads, calendars, graphics and illustrations.

Fold a standard-sized blank sheet of paper into as many pages as your newsletter has. Now arrange the material on the pages. The most important stories go on the front page. Other stories with high priorities go to the last page and to page three. Reserve the tops of pages for important items. Stories of secondary importance (including the continued portion of longer articles) go lower on pages.

A picture goes with its story. Often a picture and its caption are an entire story—and ideal as a front-page feature. Assign other material such as mastheads, calendars, etc. to key parts of pages, usually top or bottom, striving for balance and symmetry.

For instance, a picture at one corner of a page can balance a masthead at the other corner. Compare facing pages: Do they work together? That's how a reader will see them.

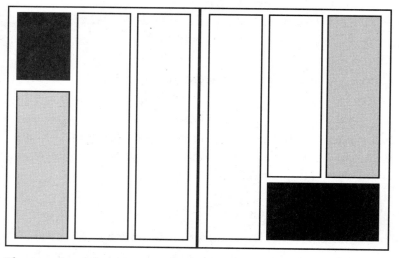

Place small and dark pieces to the outside and bottom edges of a spread.

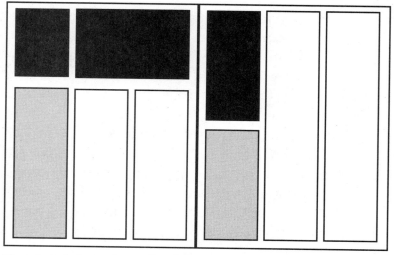

Note the imbalance the small and dark pieces create when placed on the tops and insides of the spread.

Assign headlines to stories. Use the style and size that at once reflect the importance of a story and blend with other heads on the page. Don't put two identical style heads side by side; they cancel each other out.

Nameplate

Insurance policy article

Contents box

Announcement of new office space available

Building photo

A dummy page looks like this.

JUMPING STORIES

Extra long stories may have to be jumped, i.e., continued on another page. Try to avoid jumping stories; readers tend to quit reading rather than turn the page. (Studies show that you lose as many as 83 *percent* of your readers.) But sometimes jumps are necessary.

When a story is jumped from one page to another be sure to end with a *jump line*, "continued on page 5, " and be sure there is another jump line, "continued from page 1" when the reader goes to page five. Place a teaser or pull quote near the jump line to sell the idea of turning the page.

Put *jump headlines* on the continuation of stories inside. A jump head can be the same as the headline on the front page, or a similarly worded head, possibly of a different size. The jump head can be merely a key word from the original head. If the original head is *Olympic Athletes To Be Tested for Drug Use*, the jump head could be *Athletes/Drug Use* or *Drug Use* or *Drugs*. Use anything that directs the reader to the remainder of the story.

If possible, break a jumped story in the middle of a sentence. This induces the reader to turn the page to finish the sentence at least, and perhaps the story.

Use an index on the front page to call attention to a story inside. If you have extra space on the front page, use a *solo*, i.e, a one-line head, at the top or the bottom or in a box in the middle to call attention to an important inside story.

> quam erat volupat. Ut wise enim ad minim veniam, quis nostrud exerci tation ullamcorper suscipit laboris nisl ut aliquip ex ea commodo
>
> *Find out how he turned his life around...*
> *Continued on page 3*

Encourage readers to stay with you by adding a teaser to your jump line.

MARKING SPECIFICATIONS

If you are not doing the typesetting and layout of your newsletter, you need a formal system with which to communicate specifications and changes to your desktop publisher. The dummy you create is part of the system. Marking specifications and corrections is another.

It is your job as the editor to oversee the design. While the creativity of your desktop publisher is much needed and welcome, you must also be involved in all layout decisions.

Thus, you need to "spec" the type for your newsletter. This system has been long in use for one simple reason. It works.

Specify the following information by writing it on your dummy, on each story or on a standard instruction sheet:

1. *The width of the column in picas.* Use no fractions except one-half, e.g., *30 p, 22 1/2 p.*
2. *Kind and size of type.* Use the complete name abbreviated, e.g., *12-pt Bodoni reg roman; 10-pt Bodoni light ital; 14-pt Caledonia reg roman; 18-pt Goudy bold.*
3. *Leading.* The default leading in most publishing programs for 10-point type is 12 points. (The leading space includes the space taken up by the type. Therefore the leading size will always be as big as or bigger than the type point size.) Specify 10/12 Goudy Old Style, and the copy will be set in 10-point type with two points of extra space between each line. Specify 10/11 and the copy will have one point of extra space between lines. Specify 10/10 and there will be no extra space between the lines. This type you are reading now is set 12/14.
4. *Case.* If a passage is to be set in all capital letters, write *all caps.* If it is to be set upper and lower case, write *u/lc.*
5. *Paragraph indention size.* Indicate the amount of indent you want. If you do not want paragraphs indented, write *no indent* or use the flush left bracket symbol (but be sure to add six to eight points secondary leading between

flush left paragraphs. (See *Typesetting Specifications*, next page.)

Even with the automation brought from desktop publishing, these copy editing and typesetting specifications make a difference both in the quality of your newsletter and the respect shown to you by your desktop publishers as an organized, professional editor with high standards.

ELEMENTS OF LAYOUT

How all the elements are put together on a page constitutes *layout*. The elements of a newsletter or private newspaper are: text, headlines, subheads, photographs and other illustrations, masthead, nameplate, and other special elements used in every issue.

The single most important element in page makeup is the text of the stories. Everything else on the page is there to enhance the text. Your organization's news is, after all, the reason for having your own private newspaper. The text will be of several kinds: hard news stories, feature stories, regular columns and short items and announcements.

Headlines announce the stories, set the tone of the page. They are an important page design element. They make the reader want to read on, or they herald such an onslaught of boredom that readers instinctively know to read no more. Headlines are so important in news presentation that we have devoted an entire chapter to them (see Chapter 7).

Headlines guide the reader to where the article begins. Regardless of any great ideas you have about "designing" with headlines, they should always be placed above the article they introduce. Also, headlines that run above a photo are lost on the reader, who will see the picture first and then go right on reading down the page and on to other things.

TYPESETTING SPECIFICATIONS

c/lc   Set in upper and lower case letters

≡   SET ALL CAPS (upper case)

l.c.   set all lower case

═   SET IN SMALL CAPS

ital.   Set in italics

bf.   Set boldface

reg.rom.   Set regular roman

[12/14]   Set in 12-point type on 14 points leading
flush left and ragged right

[ ]   Set with both margins justified

⊐⊏   Center

19 pi   Set 19 picas wide

21 pl   Set with longest line
no more than 21 picas wide

▢   Indent one em
(the space of one M)

▭   Indent two ems

SELECTING THE BEST PHOTOGRAPHS

If your printing method allows photographs, they can add great interest to stories, to pages. They lend reality to words, make permanent the images of important people, events and things in the world shared by your readers.

Photos must be clear and in focus, and they must add information or interest to the story they accompany. Never use a bad picture, i.e., one that is fuzzy or shot from so far away that it shows essentially nothing. Use only crisp black and white photos, and try to get photographers to approach subjects with some imagination.

Nothing is more boring than a newsletter filled with pictures of groups standing in rows, two people shaking hands and exchanging checks and documents, and lifeless mug shots. Try to get some life in photos: people walking, talking, doing something; buildings or outdoor spaces in interesting light or from unusual angles.

A note of warning: Don't rush out and buy expensive equipment that no one can handle. Get a volunteer or professional freelance photographer, or get a good basic 35mm camera that you or someone else can use easily. Don't spend hundreds or thousands of dollars on long lenses and pink filters until someone can use the basic camera competently.

Note that digital imaging technology is affordable today. These electronic cameras capture images and store them so that your computer can retrieve them directly—no need for film and processing. If you use a handful or more of photographs in each issue, it is worth a bit of research to see if these cameras are for you.

Regardless of the camera you use, when you shoot or select photographs, look for interest, action, dramatic tension, character. Here are some guidelines for photographers.

Action. Capture an animated moment in a candid shot. For action, sometimes a photo is blurred slightly, to represent rapid motion.

The blurred background suggests the motion of the swing.

Angle. Look for unusual angles to represent a fresh viewpoint. Even for something as stolid as a building, a photographer can climb to a high spot or lie down to get a dramatic angle.

Give everyday objects a new interest by taking photographs at unusual angles.

Avoid straight line group shots by positioning people at different depths in the photograph.

Comparison/Contrast. In group shots, the relative importance of group members can be expressed in unusual or striking arrangements with one person front and center and other members in the background.

To show something extremely small or large, use contrast. For example, a tiny computer chip could be photographed on a thumbnail to show its size relative to that of something the reader is familiar with.

Composition. Compose photographs to show a strong central point of interest. Some shots can be framed in foreground elements such as fence slats, tree branches, doorways.

Character. For individual portraits of story subjects, also called mug shots, take a lot of both candid and formal poses, searching for unique qualities in the character of the subject. Don't insist that subjects stare motionlessly into the camera. Let him or her talk and even move around a bit, and catch the moment when an attitude is struck.

The flowering bush frames the far away skyline.

Make a headshot friendlier by having the subject tilt his head or turn his shoulders.

If a mug shot is to accompany a regular column (such as a letter from the president) take several different photographs. Add variety to each issue by changing the photograph.

READYING PHOTOS FOR LAYOUT

Once photographs have been developed, scanned or downloaded into your computer they can often be improved before placing in the layout. This is done through cropping, sizing and editing.

Cropping. Most photos are improved by cropping, i.e., trimming off irrelevant elements or blank spaces. Cropping is a final form of composition. Look for the main point of the picture and decide what can be cut to emphasize it.

Vary sizes and shapes of photos used in page makeup. Don't hesitate to use long, narrow pictures if the subject matter lends itself to that treatment.

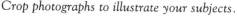

Crop photographs to illustrate your subjects.

Sizing. Photographs are often run too small in newsletters. Find the space to give good photos adequate play. Vary the sizes of photos on one page. Find the most important one and run it larger than the others. Strive for variety and emphasis.

Another note of warning: Do not run photos of yourself in your newsletter. The only exception is if you are new on the staff or are leaving and it is routine policy to run mug shots on these occasions. Never, for any reason, run more than one photograph of yourself in an issue. If you show up in the background in a good annual meeting or picnic photo, that's all right, but do not feature yourself in such photos. Professional editors do no use the newsletter as a showcase for themselves.

Printers can scale, i.e., enlarge or reduce photos to fill a space of the same proportions on the page. The space a 5x7-inch photograph will occupy can be just about any size from 2-1/2x3-1/2 inches to 8x10 inches. It is usually better to reduce than to enlarge photographs since enlarged photos can get grainy.

Using a pocket calculator or a proportion wheel (available at graphic supply stores), you can determine the final size yourself. Or establish a space of the same proportions (height to width) of the photo, and then ask the printer to reduce or enlarge the photo to fill that space. If you have a scanner and image editing software such as Adobe PhotoShop, you can size and place photos yourself.

Size photographs so that people's faces are at least as large as a thumbprint. The people in the photo on the left are hard to recognize because the thumb principle has not been followed.

Photo Editing. Almost every editor-turned-photographer has at one time taken the perfect shot of someone in their office or standing outside only to get the film back and find a tree or telephone pole growing out of the top of the person's head. That's what makes programs like Adobe PhotoShop a photo editor's dream. You can scan or download the photograph into your computer and use the image editing software to change or remove the background.

The capabilities of the software are so great that many editors struggle over whether readers should be notified if a photograph has been retouched. Most photos are retouched for aesthetic, not deceptive purposes.

The *National Geographic* was criticized because they ran a photograph in which one of the great pyramids had been *moved* in order to "balance" the frame.

You can follow guidelines set by the Associated Press and limit manipulation to standard photo methods such as cropping and adjusting contrast. The AP has decided that the content of their photographs will never be changed. Other publishers are using the label "photo illustration" or "photo montage" on extensively edited photographs.

Photo editing programs give you control over a photograph's background.

DRESSING UP PAGES

Pages can be enlivened with such design elements as screens (to make part of a black and white page a light gray), or lines, borders, boxes and so on. Your printer can help you with things like screens, or you may place them directly into the layout from your desktop publishing program. Clip art that relates to the story can be used to attract attention to the text. Drop caps or initial caps are another way to enliven an all-text page.

Use drawings, sketches and clip art that are appropriate to the quality and tone of the image you want the newsletter to project. Books and collections of clip art on disk can be purchased by direct mail or at art supply stores. These also include other design elements such as borders, maps and flags. See Appendix 5 for a listing of clip art suppliers.

Once you have prepared all the material for your newsletter, prepared the dummies and created final layout, you're ready for final production... almost.

Come to Casino Night... your ship just may come in

Lorem ipsum dolor sit amet, con secteteur adipsicing elit, sed diam nonnumy nibh euisnod tempor inci dunt ut labore et dolore magna ali quam erat volupat. Ut wise enim ad minim veniam, quis nostrud exerci tation ullamcorper suscipit laboris nisl ut aliquip ex ea commodo con sequat. Duis autem vel eum irure dolor in henderit in vulputate velit esse consequat.

Vel illum dolor eu feugiat mulla facilis at vero eos et accusm et ius to odio dignessim qui blandt prae sent luptatum zzril delenit aigue duos dolore et mosestias exceptur sint

occaecat cupidtat not simil pro vident tempor sunt in culpa qui officia desrunt mollit aniom ib est abor un et dolor fuga. Et harumd dereud facilis est er expedit distint. Nam liber tempor cum soluta nobis eligent option congue nibil impediet doming id quod maxim plecat facer possum omnis voluptas assumenda est, mnis repellend.

Temporibud auteui quinsud et aur offik debit aut tum rerum necessit atib saepe evenit ut er mosit non recusand. Itaque earun rerum hic ten tury sapiente delectus au aut perfer zim edndis dolorib asperiore repellat.

Clip art draws attention to and enlivens a newsletter page.

Chapter 11

Production
& Distribution

*The common goal is to see that
your newsletter is at its best
as it goes forth into the world.*

PREVENTIVE CARE

As the newsletter exits the layout phase, the editor's job is not yet completed. Many a beautiful newsletter creation has been crushed by poor printing or torn up in the automated machines at the post office. Many an editor has been haunted by hidden typographical errors, layout or output problems or a last-minute correction that shifted the entire layout helter-skelter.

WHAT DO GOOD PROOFREADERS DO?

While the editor proofreads during the editing stage, one last proof-reading session is in order. At this point, a volunteer or paid proof-reader saves you hours of agony. You're too close to the project to see the obvious.

A good proofreader, like some good mothers we have known, worries a lot. The common goal is to see that your newsletter is at its best as it goes forth into the world; the mode of operation is to check that everything that can be done has been done to help. Proofreaders' special marks—see page 166—tell the story: they worry about everything.

First are the omissions, generally classifiable as *misses*: misspellings, misalignments, mispagination, missing words and letters, missing punctuation, missing sentences, missing sense. Then there are, conversely, those things that should not have been done that have been done and that show up on the page as party crashers, *extras*: extra spaces between words or lines, extra words or letters anywhere, extra type styles and sizes.

Proofreading to ferret out just such errors as these has been a part of printing since Gutenberg perfected moveable type, and some consideration of that history may give you heart. A sixteenth century proofreader, Jerome Hornschuch, suffered much in his profession. "Every day I had to struggle...with incorrect and revolting copy....in a book the other day...I had to mark nearly two thousand errors: so I began to consider how a check could be put to this..."

He wrote a book—the first proofreader's manual. He emphasized that correctors must be sober (that is, not drunk), that their rooms should be well-lighted. The corrector "must have a quick eye for minute detail, understand words and form and paging....must proof-read aloud with a reading boy." Particulars to watch for, he wrote, are "beginnings and ends of lines, clear type (not smudged or broken), the right font and correct spacing." He printed proofmarks in use today. The year was 1608.

While the computer age much admires itself as helpful with proofreading tasks such as spelling, the "spell checks" available on even the best software are partial and inconsistent. Even given that their irrational responses are good for many laughs, spell checks are not ideal companions. As one 18th century author said of the gentleman "corrector" engaged to proofread his work: "...he Confounds rather than Corrects and must not be depended upon, and if he is not to be depended upon I see no use there is of him."

We will defend the Corrector and his descendant "spell checks" by saying that they do catch many errors; the key word is *depend*. One must not depend on them to catch every error. Word processing makes quick corrections possible: words, sentences, whole paragraphs and pages can be changed or moved at the touch of a few keys.

With this advantage comes equal opportunity for stupendous error. At the touch of one wrong key, those same words, sentences, paragraphs and pages will show up in strange places, in strange forms—or disappear entirely. If the writer does not catch these errors, the proofreader must. Else the printed result may have—as one 17th century editor complained after his printer had botched the job—"more faults than lines."

Once you're certain the layout is error-free, you're ready for mass production.

PROOFREADING CHECKLIST

Newsletter: _____

Issue/Date: _____

Text:

- ❑ Read everything once through for overall feel
- ❑ Read through for punctuation and spelling
- ❑ Read all articles and headlines aloud
- ❑ Look at headlines only
- ❑ Read headlines and most visible text backwards
  (*Forces the eye to concentrate on the words instead of reading the sentence.*)
- ❑ Check spelling of all names and company names
- ❑ Call phone numbers to verify
- ❑ Confirm date of newsletter
- ❑ Confirm date of copyright
- ❑ Other:
- ❑ Other:
- ❑ Other:

Layout:

- ❑ Artwork straight
- ❑ Typefaces correct
- ❑ Bulk rate indicia included (if used)
- ❑ Consistent spacing between elements (headline & body copy, column width, etc.)
- ❑ Phone number and contact information included where needed
- ❑ Other:
- ❑ Other:
- ❑ Other:

Printer's Proofs/Bluelines:

- ❑ No specks or unusual marks
- ❑ Photographs in correct place
- ❑ Correct crop and screen on photos
- ❑ Color break correct (if printing in more than one color)
- ❑ Other:
- ❑ Other:

Make a checklist to ferret out your common proofreading errors.

COPYEDITING & PROOFREADING MARKS

Mark	Meaning	Example
⌐σ	delete; take out	Always mark all proofs.
#	insert space	Always mark proofs properly.
∧	insert letter(s) or word(s)	Always mak proofs properly.
∿ᵗⁿ	transpose letters or words	Always proofs mark properly.
⊂	close up; no space	Always m ark proofs properly.
⊏	align with left margin	⌜Always mark proofs properly.
⊐	align with right margin	⌝Always mark proofs properly.
⊐⊏	center	⌝ Mark Proofs ⌐
¶	start new paragraph	¶Always mark proofs properly.
no ¶	do not start new paragraph	Always mark proofs. Mark them properly. *no ¶*
∼	do not start new line	Always mark proofs properly.
stet	do not make correction; let stand as written	Always mark proofs properly. stet
qv.	this is wrong; see copy	Alsays proper mark poof qv.
?	this is questionable; check or query author	Never mark proofs properly. ?
∧	insert comma	Proofs if properly marked.
⊙	insert period	Always mark proofs properly⊙
ⱽ	insert apostrophe	The proofs in the proof marks.
ⱽ	insert quotation marks	He said, Mark proofs properly.
=/	insert hyphen	The writer editor marks proofs
(− −)	insert dash	Always not sometimes mark
SP	spell out	Proofing is a No. 1 priority. SP
//	align	Always mark proofs properly

Cost-Effective Printing

If you need only a small number of copies, you'll probably copy the newsletter yourself or, if you do not have access to a good copying machine, have your instant printer do it.

If you want to use a printer, however, get bids. Make a list of specifications, including the exact number of copies needed, the dimensions of the pages, the number of pages, the number of photos in an average issue, the paper stock and color, and the color or colors of ink you want. (More than one color will drive costs substantially higher.) If you want the printer to cut, collate, staple and fold the newsletters, put those operations on the list. You can make up your own bid sheets, get them from a printer, buy them from an art supply store or use the form in this book (see Appendix 4). The important thing is to put specifications in writing.

Establish a clear understanding with your printer. A relationship of mutual trust and understanding saves time and trouble for you both. It is good to work with the same printer issue after issue. But when you contract with a printer for services, put in a clause permitting you to cancel if the printer consistently fails to deliver on time or to meet standards of quality. Be clear about a fixed cost for standard specifications (as noted on the bid sheet), but allow some flexibility for one-time changes and variations.

Look at samples of the printer's work, and talk to some of his active customers. Don't make cost the sole deciding factor in choosing a printer. Expect to do your part in building a good working relationship. Don't put pressure on him by constantly missing your own deadlines. He may be able to bail you out sometimes; at other times he won't.

If you remain flexible in your approach, you'll find that the printer can show you ways to save time and money by altering specifications. Show your printer a dummy or sketch of your newsletter. Encourage the printer to suggest ways to hold down or trim costs. Sometimes a printer will have enough paper left over from a large job that can be used for your newsletter—and will cost less than custom-ordered paper. A slight variation in paper weight or texture will probably not visibly affect the appearance of your publication.

If black and white begins to bore you, use a light-colored paper—it is much less expensive than running the pages through the press a second time to get a second color of ink. Beware of papers so dark that they muddy photographs and make print hard to read.

When deciding on the number of copies to make or order, allow for standard circulation plus extras for file or future use. A special story in an issue may be reason to print additional extra copies for special distribution. Look at the content of each issue and try to anticipate any clamor from the public to get copies of it.

DISTRIBUTING YOUR NEWS

Small circulation employee newsletters are often distributed by hand to employees at work. This method of distribution creates interaction and dialogue among fellow workers and provides immediate feedback.

But it has drawbacks. The newsletter is read hastily at work, if at all. Employees who do read it thoroughly lose productive time on the job. There's less chance the newsletter will be taken home—there to be read by family and friends. To gain advantages, some organizations mail newsletters to employees at home.

Newsletters for customers, association members and donors are usually mailed.

KEEPING UP WITH YOUR MAILING LIST

Organizations that mail newsletters must keep good mailing lists. Keeping lists up-to-date can entail much time and effort. The costs of postage and time spent on maintaining lists are major expenses in newsletter publishing.

Labels for reader lists of fewer than 500 names can be most economically and efficiently handled by using the office copier to make new sets of pressure-sensitive labels. This works especially well if the mailing list changes little and if the names do not have to be sorted by zip code.

For lists of more than 2,000, using computer labels can be cost-efficient. Organizations with their own computers often handle their own mailing lists. For those without computers, most larger cities have computer firms that handle mailing lists.

The big cost is the initial one. But after names have been entered into the computer, the costs of adding and deleting names and of generating labels for each issue are nominal.

Mailing Through the Post Office

There are four ways to mail newsletters.

First Class. This is the most expensive, especially if your newsletter weighs more than an ounce. But it gets priority handling, and if getting the newsletter to readers quickly is essential, it may be the best way. Address corrections on first class mailings are free of charge and help you keep up with migrating readers.

Second Class. This is the cheapest way to mail newsletters but there are numerous requirements for qualifying for a second class permit. The newsletter must be published regularly and have a publication office that is open during regular business hours. It must have a list of paid subscribers and be devoted primarily to news, not advertising. It must contain an identification statement within its first five pages. The cost of the permit depends on the size of the circulation.

Third Class Bulk Rate. To qualify for a third class bulk rate permit, the mailing must be at least 200 pieces. There is a yearly fee plus a one-time only fee for the permit holder. Newsletters must be sorted by zip code, bundled and bagged according to specific rules.

If you use third class bulk rate, it is a good idea to include your own name and address on the mailing list. You'll get a pretty good idea of when the newsletter is received by subscribers, which may be several days after delivery to the post office.

When using second or third class, preprint your postal permit indicia on the mailing space of your newsletter. It saves the time of putting on stamps and the cost of using envelopes.

Postal regulations and costs change continually and often affect size and printing standards. Ask local postal authorities to notify you of any changes.

For all but very small circulations, preparing newsletters for bulk mailing by hand can be time-consuming. Most mailing operations can be done by machine—folding, stuffing, sealing, stamping and addressing.

Calculate the cost per copy of doing this job yourself, including the wages of persons on the staff who do it. Chances are, the job can be farmed out to a mailing service that uses machines for less than it is costing you now.

Chapter 12

Editors
of the Future

*Technology frees your time for the real job
of news editing—getting out the news in
appropriately written style to a
finely targeted audience.*

FROM DESKTOP TO ONLINE

Revolutions in publishing technology, including desktop publishing and the storm of paperless publishing on the Worldwide Web and intra-company networks, will continue to have a great impact on the way we produce newsletters.

Many a reluctant editor has shelved the beloved typewriters, Xacto knives and rubber cement and taken the dive into the world of desktop publishing. Soon, these same editors will be seeing less and less of their laser printers as they write and format their news for distribution via modem or fax.

Though many of the online materials end up being printed by the user, paperless technology saves by having people actively search and retrieve only what they need. This, in comparison to mass mailings that only a small percentage of recipients read, has direct impact on valuable resources such as postage and paper. It also has implications for how you write your newsletter.

"PULL" VERSUS "PUSH" COMMUNICATIONS

For 500 years publishers have been *pushing* printed materials at readers in hopes that they will be read. The electronic age is centered more around readers *pulling* what they want.

On the Internet, publications are uploaded (copied onto the network system) and available for any reader who wants to *pull* them off. Fax-on-demand systems are another example of pull communications. The readers call your fax-on-demand system, enter their fax numbers and select the documents they want to receive.

All of these technologies have interesting implications for newsletters. Editors must rethink how to present their publications. Giving readers the precise content that they want (which, by the way, is a good idea no matter what) becomes crucial.

How you write your headlines will make or break an electronic newsletter. Readers—who are paying for the phone or online charges—will be quickly scanning the options and selecting only the most interesting files. Your headlines must be active, show direct reader benefit and arouse curiosity. (Again, a good idea no matter how you produce your newsletter but crucial online and with fax-on-demand systems.)

For those of you on CompuServe, Prodigy, America Online or any of the other services, start paying attention to the library files with the most downloads. They have great headlines. These headlines are also severely restricted in word count.

GOOD JOURNALISM IS STILL GOOD JOURNALISM

Remember how desktop publishing opened up a new variety of possibilities for your page layout? Online publishing does the same for how you present information.

No longer does your news have to go in a two-dimensional, *start in the front and work toward the back* form. This gives you unseen benefits. For example, a company making filtration systems could introduce a new filter and also show how it works using three-dimensional and animated graphics. The announcement could be set up as a video presentation along with voice and other sounds.

That said, your challenges as an "onscreen" journalist follow the same guidelines set forth in the pages of this book. All technology does is ease the distribution of the products of your news editing. Your goal remains the same—*spread the news in an appropriately written style to a carefully targeted audience.*

Appendix 1

Publication Guidelines

1. MISSION STATEMENT

Every newsletter may be said to have its own mission—the purpose and scope envisioned for the newsletter by the organization responsible for its publication. To define that mission clearly, write it down in a *mission statement*, outlining the following points:

1.1   What is the purpose of the newsletter?

1.2   Who is the intended reader?

1.3   What is its geographical reach?

1.4   What is the desired writing style?

1.5   What is the frequency?

1.6   What articles will appear in every issue? How long will they be? (List each with approximate word count.)

1.7   Who has approval on newsletter content and final approval on each issue's writing and layout?

2. GUIDELINES FOR SUBMITTED ARTICLES

2.1   Write to fit space for _____ words.

2.2   Check grammar, spelling, punctuation and figures for accuracy.

2.3   Write a suggested headline in active tense (when appropriate) and include verbs in all headlines. Write kickers and decks when assigned.

2.4   Complete a story in all respects before turning it in.

2.5   The deadline for submission is _____ .

2.6   Include all photographs and art work. If they are unavoidably delayed, list them and describe their contents and intended use in the story. Write suggested captions for all visuals.

2.7   Submit the article on disk along with a printout. Make a copy for your own files.

Format requested is_____ .

3. Guidelines for Illustrations & Photographs

3.1   The photograph or illustration will occupy approximately _____ x _____ space in the newsletter.

3.2   When submitting photographs on disk, please save in _____ (format). When submitting illustrations on disk, please save in _____ (format).

3.3   Please illustrate _____ (subject).

3.4   Special instructions or information on backgrounds: _____

3.5   The deadline is _____ .

4. Layout Style Sheet

Typefaces

4.1   <u>Headlines</u>. Important news stories are: _____

Secondary news stories are: _____

Sidebar and other headlines are: _____

Short news item headlines are: _____

Subheads are: _____

4.2   Body copy is: _____

4.3   Captions are: _____

4.4   Decks are: _____

4.5   Kickers or standing heads are: _____

4.6   Drop or initial caps are: _____

4.7   Nameplate text is: _____

4.8   Masthead text is: _____

4.9   Pull quotes are: _____

Format

4.10 Number of pages:_____

4.11 Paper size:_____

4.12 Page size:_____

4.13 Folded to:_____ (size)

4.14 Paper:_____

4.15 Ink colors:_____

4.16 Screens are:_____

4.17 Margins:_____

4.18 Indents are:_____

4.19 Number of columns:_____

4.20 Distance between columns:_____

4.21 Column rules are:_____

4.22 Justified or ragged right text:_____

4.23 Distance between headlines and body copy:_____

Appendix 2

Model Stylebook

1. PUNCTUATION

The Period

1.1 The period is used after a declarative or imperative sentence: *There are 50 states. Count the people.*

1.2 The period is used in abbreviations: *the U.S., the U.N.*

1.3 The period is sometimes used after a statement that includes an implicit question: *I don't know why he would do that.*

The Comma

1.4 The comma separates words and figures to avoid confusion: *What the solution is, is a question. August 1, 1984. There are 18,758 fans at the Grackles' game tonight.*

1.5 The comma separates items in a series: *The woman was tall, dark, and handsomely dressed.* If the last two items in a series are single words, the comma is not used because it is clearly not needed to clarify meaning: *Hooray for the red, white and blue!*

1.6 The comma is used before *and, but, or, for* and *nor* when those connectives introduce second independent clauses into a sentence: *The day's cool, hazy atmosphere made her tired, but he was as full of energy as ever.*

   If they do not, the comma is omitted: *The city slept and at the same time, exuded a kind of dull energy.* Short main clauses may be separated by commas: *He ran, I rode my bike.*

1.7 The comma is used to set off nonrestrictive material: *His uncle, a good man, disliked cats. The work, he discovered, was exhausting.*

1.8 The comma should not separate a subject from its verb or a verb from its object.

The Semicolon

1.9   The semicolon separates two medium-length or long independent clauses: *The drapes in the living room were hideous; they seemed to have been chosen by someone from outer space.* It is used to separate two such clauses introduced by connectives such as *and, or, but, for* and *nor* when the independent clauses they introduce are complex or have commas in them.

1.10   Semicolons are used for items in a series that have commas within them: *The party consisted of R. G. Austin; Sally Austin, his wife; Jane Austin, his mother; Anna Rabbit, her nurse; and Giles, the chauffeur.* (Without the semicolons, this could read as eight people; and, in fact, without the semicolon, it would be impossible to determine for sure who the various characters and roles in this lineup are.)

The Apostrophe

1.11   The apostrophe indicates the possessive case of nouns: *Joel's graduation, Crosby's son, the couple's dog, boys' wear, states' rights.*

1.12   The apostrophe is not used to indicate the possessive *its. The cat was playing with its yarn.* An apostrophe and *s* used with it means *it is. It's a great day for singing a song.*

1.13   There are some unusual applications of apostrophe use: *for Jesus' sake, the Joneses' house, Moses' tablet.*

1.14   The apostrophe indicates the omission of figures: *class of '84, the fabulous '50s.*

1.15   When the apostrophe is not an official part of a name, don't use it: *Johns Hopkins University, Actors Equity Association.* Use it according to tradition: *the Court of St. James's.*

The Colon

1.16 The colon introduces summary matter: lists, statements and conclusions that follow from preceding matter. It takes the place of an implied example: *After months of agonizing, he reached a decision: he couldn't make a decision. The $1,000,000 was left to his survivors: $999,000 to his dog, $1,000 to his son.*

1.17 The colon is used for Biblical and academic references: *Matthew 2:14. Gastroenterology 1980; 79:311-14.*

The Exclamation Point

1.18 The exclamation point is used to indicate enthusiasm, surprise, incredulity or another strong emotion: *How wonderful! What! Come back here!* The exclamation point is fundamentally out of place in news writing.

Parentheses

1.19 Parentheses set off closely related, nonrestrictive material from the text: *It is not the custom (at least in the areas he mentioned) to stand at attention during political speeches. "That idea," he said, "as explained by (Rep. Frank) Wright, is very appealing."*

1.20 When location identification is needed but is not part of an official group name, parentheses are used: *The Kansas City (MO) Historical Society.* They are not appropriately used to separate parts of essential information from each other: *The Kansas City, Kansas area population is 234,000.*

1.21 When the last part of a sentence is parenthetical, the punctuation goes outside the parentheses: *We will be living in Paris this fall (we hope, we hope). Nine persons out of ten eat curds and whey (see Figure 3).*

1.22   A complete sentence may be parenthesized, in which case it takes its punctuation with it: *The Spruce Goose is the largest airplane ever built. (Its wingspan is longer than two football fields!)*

Quotation Marks

1.23   Quotation marks enclose direct statements by a person other than the writer: *He said, "Read it; it will change your life."* In quotes that are several paragraphs long, each paragraph begins with quotation marks, but closing quote marks are used only once—at the end of the last paragraph.

1.24   Quotation marks are used on slang expressions, on words used as words in typewritten copy, and misnomers. They are sometimes used to show the writer's intent to be ironic: *She was "too busy" to visit her mother.*

1.25   In typewritten copy, use quotation marks on titles of books, plays, poems, movies, speeches, etc. In typeset copy, however, italicize such titles. Exceptions are speeches, short musical compositions, and titles of paintings and other works of art, which take quotation marks.

1.26   Use quotation marks on nicknames: *Jim "Moondog" Morey and Phil "Monsoon" McManus spent the evening listening to Richard "Little Richey" Lucente's Cajun band.*

1.27   Commas and periods are placed inside closing quotation marks; colons and semicolons are placed outside them. Other punctuation is placed according to meaning: *Why call it a "gentleman's agreement"? The question is, "Should we get married?" Doesn't her habit of saying "You know?" all the time bother you?*

1.28   Quotes within quotes are identified by double, then single marks, thus: "The question is, 'If you're so smart, then why aren't you rich?' "

The Dash

1.29 The dash indicates a sudden intrusion of a thought
related to the subject. *He claimed—no one denied it—that
he had trouble hearing her. If that man should ever really
listen—God forbid!—he might understand her.*

(When typesetting, do not space before and after the
dash. Use the kerning feature of your publishing software
to keep the dash from butting against the letters.)

The Hyphen

1.30 The hyphen forms compound words and expressions:
A-bomb, 20-20 vision, secretary-treasurer.

1.31 The hyphen is used suspensively, to attach more than
one adjective to a noun in such expressions as *low-to-
moderate-income housing ... 14- and 15-year-olds.* (Note
the space left before the *and.*)

1.32 When a prefix ends in and is followed by the same letter,
a hyphen is sometimes used: *post-traumatic.* Check a
current dictionary for hyphenation. Exceptions are
many: *preempt, reelect, cooperate, coed, coordinate.* Prefixes such as *demi, semi, bi, tri, co, pre, re, sub, super,
inter, intra, anti, over* and *under* are usually joined to a
word without a hyphen.

1.33 The hyphen is not used with adverbs. Do not use it with
words ending in *ly: badly damaged, fully informed.*

1.34 The hyphen may serve to distinguish meanings of identi-
cally spelled words: *recover, re-cover, resent, re-sent.*

1.35 The hyphen separates a prefix from a capitalized proper
noun: *un-American, pre-Norman.*

1.36 The prefix *ex* is hyphenated: *ex-wife, ex-officio.*

1.37 Fractions are hyphenated: *one and one-half years ago,
10 one-and-one-half-year-olds.*

1.38 Do not hyphenate words formed with the suffixes *like* or
wide: childlike, citywide.

1.39 Do not hyphenate such combinations as *vice president* and *surgeon general*.

1.40 Hyphenate nouns that express a double occupation: *writer-editor, architect-planner*.

Italics

1.41 Use italics in typeset roman copy to identify words, phrases and letters meant to stand out from the rest of the text. In italic text, use roman type to make words stand out. Mind your *p*'s and *q*'s; *Mind your* p's *and* q's. I am reading *Ulysses*; *I am reading* Ulysses.

2. Capitalization

2.1 Capitalize a title preceding a name: *Board Chairman Ella Ross*. But do not capitalize such titles when they stand alone or follow a name: *Benoit Guin, executive director*.

2.2 Capitalize official titles used before names: *Mayor Charles Wheeler, Governor Joseph Teasdale*. But write: *the mayor, the governor; Charles Wheeler, mayor of Kansas City; John Carlin, governor of Kansas; Charles Price, ambassador to England*, or *the ambassador*.

2.3 Do not capitalize long titles that follow a name: *Alan Doan, first vice president in charge of marketing*.

2.4 Do not capitalize occupational titles such as *pianist Olga Peterson, rookie left-handed pitcher Bill Lafferty, defense attorney Tom Loughlin*. (Do not separate such titles from names with a comma.)

2.5 Capitalize *U.S. Congress, Iowa Senate, Maine Legislature*. But write: *The state legislature passed the bill*. (Note: the building is the Capitol; the city is the capital.)

2.6 Capitalize *the States* when referring to the United States, but do not capitalize *national, federal* or *government* used as adjectives: *the national group, the legislative body*.

Capitalize *State* used as part of an official title: *State Highway Department.* But write *the state, the region, the county* and *the city* in later references.

2.7 Capitalize the names of federal legislative bodies and committees: *Congress, Senate, House, U.S. Foreign Affairs Committee.* Do not capitalize adjective forms such as *congressional, legislative* and *senatorial.* Write *the committee* in later references, once the full title is established in a story.

2.8 Capitalize *Social Security Administration.* But write: *He was an advocate of social security.*

2.9 Capitalize *U.S. Army, U.S. Navy, U.S. Marines,* but write: *the army, the navy, the marines* and *soldier, sailor, marine.*

2.10 Capitalize holiday names, historic events, observation weeks, hurricanes: *Labor Day, Easter, National Safety Week, Hurricane Bob.*

2.11 Capitalize specific regions: *Middle East, Midwest, Arctic Circle, Upper Peninsula, the Orient, the East* (meaning the Orient). But do not capitalize words that merely indicate direction: *It is east of here, west of there, in the northern part of the state, on the east coast.*

2.12 Capitalize names of political parties, social and fraternal organizations: *Republican, Kappa Kappa Gamma, Knights of Columbus.*

2.13 Capitalize names of people and races: *Caucasian, Asian, Chinese, African American, Native American, Cajun.*

2.14 Capitalize a common noun used in a formal name: *Hoover Dam, Missouri River, Cassidy County Courthouse, Wall Street.* But write *the dam, the river, the courthouse* and *the street* in later references.

2.15 Capitalize trade names and use trade or registration marks with them on first reference: *Xerox®, Q-tips®* .

2.16   Capitalize titles of books, plays, poems, paintings: *Paris Was Yesterday, A Chorus Line, The Road Not Taken,* "The Girl in White" (painting).

2.17   Capitalize the first word of a quote introduced by a comma or a colon only if the quote is a complete sentence. *Franklin said, "A penny saved is a penny earned." Did Hamlet say, "O that this too, too sullied flesh would melt"? He said the plan was "ridiculous beyond belief."*

2.18   Capitalize Biblical references and fanciful appellations and award names: *the Bible, a Biblical character, Buckeye State, Show-me State, Operation Breakthrough, Medal of Honor, Nobel Peace Prize.*

2.19   Do not capitalize *plan, report, project* or *study* unless the word is part of an official title.

3. SPELLING

The neutral, central vowel sound of most unstressed syllables in American English is the *schwa* (symbol ə). If it can be said to be pronounced at all, it is pronounced as a very weak *uh* sound: *ago, agent, maintenance, incredible, bachelor.* The only guide to spelling words containing schwas is to memorize them. Try a mnemonic (memory-aiding) device such as magnifying in your mind the syllable containing the schwa: *baLANCE, indepenDENT, eliGIBLE, sponSOR, foREIGN.*

3.1   Words like *niece, receive* and *friend* are frequently misspelled. The order of the vowels in the *ie* combination is generally stated in the jingle: "Write *i* before *e* except after *c* or when sounded as *ay* as in *neighbor* and *weigh.*"

Some other common words spelled with *ei* are *counterfeit, either, foreign, forfeit, height, heir, leisure, neither, seize* and *sovereign.*

3.2   *Homonyms* sound alike but have different meanings and, usually, different spellings: *altar* and *alter, peace* and *piece, weak* and *week*. A writer working fast and thinking phonetically may use the spelling of one when he or she intends the other; *their* and *there* are often confused. The spell-check cannot catch these.

Here are some pairs of homonyms that give frequent trouble: *affect (to produce an effect upon)* and *effect (to make, or as a noun, roughly, result)*; *all together (all at once)* and *altogether (wholly or thoroughly)*; *canvas (cloth)* and *canvass (to solicit)*; *council (group)* and *counsel (to advise or, as a noun, lawyer)*; *forward (ahead)* and *foreword (preface)*; *its (belonging to it)* and *it's (it is)*; *precede (to go or come before)* and *proceed (to move along a course)*; *who's (who is)* and *whose (belonging to whom)*.

3.3   Since most English nouns take s plurals, all plurals formed in any other way are considered irregular. The troublesome plurals are those ending in o or y. Such nouns have regular s plurals when the o or y immediately follows a vowel: *cameos, keys, attorneys, donkeys, valleys, folios, radios, studios*. They are generally irregular when the o or y follows a consonant: *buffaloes, cargoes, echoes, heroes, potatoes, torpedoes, vetoes*.
The chief exceptions are musical terms: *altos, bassos, pianos, solos, sopranos*. Others are *autos, cantos, dynamos, Eskimos, mementos, provisos* and *quartos*.
Plurals of nouns ending in a consonant plus y are formed by changing the y to i before adding es: *allies, babies, cities, cries, tries*.

3.4   Plurals of nouns ending in s, ss, sh, ch, x or z are formed by simply adding es: *Jameses, ashes, bunches, taxes, foxes, buzzes*. Some exceptions: *bass, fish, perch, ellipses, theses*.

3.5   In words of one syllable, the final consonant is usually doubled before a suffix beginning with a vowel if the word ends in a single consonant and contains a single vowel: *war, warring, tap, tapped*.

This rule extends to words of more than one syllable if the accent falls on the last syllable: *preFER, preferred, BENefit, benefited; conFER, conferring.*

3.6   When a suffix beginning with a consonant is added to a word ending in a silent *e*, the *e* is retained: *achievement,extremely, indefinitely, sincerely.* Exceptions: *argument, awful, duly, ninth, probably, wholly.* *Abridgment, acknowledgment* and *judgment* are preferred to the also acceptable spellings *abridgement, acknowledgement* and *judgement.*

3.7   When a suffix beginning with a vowel is added to a word ending in silent *e*, the *e* is dropped unless it is required to indicate pronunciation or to avoid confusion with a similar word: *accumulating, achieving, boring, coming, grievance, icy.* Exceptions are: (to keep a *c* or *g* soft): *advantageous, changeable, courageous, manageable, noticeable, outrageous, peaceable, serviceable, singeing, tingeing, vengeance;* (to prevent mispronunciation), *canoeist, eyeing, hoeing, mileage, shoeing;* (to prevent confusion with other words) *dyeing.*

3.8   Words ending with the sound *seed* are usually spelled *cede: accede, concede, intercede, precede, recede, secede.* There are exceptions: *exceed, proceed, succeed, supersede.*

3.9   Here are some often used and frequently misspelled words:

accommodate	exhilarate	irrelevant
paralleled	siege	acknowledgment
existence	judgment	Philippines
skillful	adviser	fulfill
liaison	Portuguese	stabilize
all right	guerrilla	lightning
privilege	tranquility	bouillon
gypsy	liquefy	resistance
vilify	canister	harass
marshal	restaurateur	weird
diarrhea	hemorrhage	minuscule

salable	ecstasy	inoculate
nickel	scurrilous	embarrass
iridescent	niece	sergeant

3.10 Most prefixes and suffixes are written *solid*, i.e., without the hyphen. Exceptions are noted. Some general rules for prefixes and suffixes:

all (hyphenated): *all-star*
ante, anti: *antebellum, antiestablishment* (except in proper noun usage such as *anti-American*)
bi: *biennial, bifocal*
co: *copilot, coed* but *co-worker*
counter: *counterfoil, counteract*
down: *downstroke, touchdown*
electro: *electrolysis, electrolyte*
ex (hyphenated): *ex-champion*
extra: *extraterrestrial, extramarital*
fold: *twofold*
in (prefix): *insufferable*; (suffix hyphenated): *stand-in*
infra: *infrared*
inter: *interstate, intergalactic*
intra: *intrastate, intramural*
multi: *multimillion, multifaceted*
non: *nonpartisan, nonsupport*
out: (hyphenated): *out-talk, out-box*
over: *overcome, pushover*
post: *postwar, postpartum*
pre: *predetermine, prewar*
self (hyphenated): *self-defense, self-respect*
semi: *semiannual*
sub: *subfreezing*
super: *superabundant*
trans: *transatlantic, transcontinental* (but *trans-American*)
tri: *trifocal*
ultra: *ultraviolet*
un: *unshaven, unnecessary* (but *un-American*)
under: *underground, undersold*
wide: *areawide, worldwide*

4. ABBREVIATIONS

4.1   In first mention, names of organizations should be spelled out (*American Medical Association, Centers for Disease Control*), and the abbreviation should follow the name in parentheses. Thereafter in the story, the abbreviation may be used:

The Kansas City Metropolitan Region (KCMR) includes two more counties than the city's Standard Metropolitan Statistical Area (SMSA).

The report was submitted to the Department of Housing and Urban Development (HUD).

Note: Periods are not used in most such abbreviations.

4.2   Abbreviate St., Ave., Blvd., Ter., in addresses, but not Point, Port, Circle, Plaza, Place, Drive, Oval, Road, Lane: *16 E. 72nd St.; 16 Gregory Ave. NW* (no periods in NW); *Sunset Boulevard, Main Street, Fifth Avenue* (where no specific address is given). Highways are written as numbers: *I-35, US 69, US 71 Bypass, M-7, K-10.*

4.3   Lower case abbreviations usually take periods. The rule is that if the letters form words, periods are needed: *c.o.d., f.o.b.*

4.4   Traditional abbreviations for the states as still observed in news writing (by *The New York Times* e.g.) are: Ala. (for Alabama)*, Ariz., Ark., Calif., Colo., Conn., Del., Fla., Ga., Ia., Ill., Ind., Kans., Ky., La., Md., Mass., Mich., Minn., Miss., Mo., Mont., Neb., Nev., N.C., N.D., N.H., N.J., N.M., N.Y., Okla., Ore., Pa., R.I., S.C., S.D., Tenn., Tex., Vt., Va., Wash., Wis., W.Va., and Wyo.

*Alaska, Hawaii, Idaho, Iowa, Ohio, Maine and Utah are not abbreviated in news writing.

The commonwealth of Puerto Rico is P.R.; the

Virgin Islands, V.I. States are not given at all for large cities such as New York, Washington, Chicago and Seattle. Nations are not given for internationally known cities such as Paris and Berlin.

The U.S. Postal Service two-letter abbreviations for the states and the territories are not used in newswriting. But they should be used on your mailing lists. In some very polite circles, state names in addresses are still abbreviated as above, or even spelled out; but it is only practical to succumb to U.S.P.S. usage in order to get the mail where you want it to go.

A few words about the U.S.P.S. system: Note that periods are not used even for two-word states like ND or WV or for DC. And if you believe that logic will help you determine abbreviations you do not know, look at those for Maine or the territories.

Alabama	AL
Alaska	AK
Arizona	AZ
Arkansas	AR
American Samoa	AS
California	CA
Colorado	CO
Connecticut	CT
Delaware	DE
District of Columbia	DC
Federated States of Micronesia	TT
Florida	FL
Georgia	GA
Guam	GU
Hawaii	HI
Idaho	ID
Illinois	IL
Indiana	IN
Iowa	IA
Kansas	KS

Kentucky	KY
Louisiana	LA
Maine	ME
Marshall Islands	TT
Maryland	MD
Massachusetts	MA
Michigan	MI
Minnesota	MN
Mississippi	MS
Missouri	MO
Montana	MT
Nebraska	NE
Nevada	NV
New Hampshire	NH
New Jersey	NJ
New Mexico	NM
New York	NY
North Carolina	NC
North Dakota	ND
Northern Mariana Islands	CM
Ohio	OH
Oklahoma	OK
Oregon	OR
Palau	TT
Pennsylvania	PA
Puerto Rico	PR
Rhode Island	RI
South Carolina	SC
South Dakota	SD
Tennessee	TN
Texas	TX
Utah	UT
Vermont	VT
Virginia	VA
Virgin Islands	VI
Washington	WA
West Virginia	WV
Wisconsin	WI
Wyoming	WY

4.5 Abbreviate *United Nations* and *United States* in titles: *U.S. Chamber of Commerce*. Otherwise spell them out.

4.6 Abbreviate and capitalize religious, fraternal, scholastic or honorary degrees, but use lower case when they are spelled out: *B.S.*, *bachelor of science*.

4.7 Abbreviate and capitalize titles such as: *Mr.*, *Mrs.*, *Ms.*, *Mlle.*, *Dr.*, *Prof.*, *Sen.*, *Rep.*, *Asst.*, *Lt. Gov.*, *Gen.*, *Supt.*, *Atty. Gen.* before names but not after. *President* is not abbreviated in any use.

4.8 Do not abbreviate months in sentences; write *October 12, 1942*. Abbreviations used in tabular matter are: *Jan.*, *Feb.*, *Mar.*, *Apr.*, *Jun.*, *Jul.*, *Aug.*, *Sept.*, *Oct.*, *Nov.*, *Dec. May* requires no abbreviation.

4.9 Days of the week are abbreviated only in tabular matter, where they are: *Mon.*, *Tue.*, *Wed.*, *Thu.*, *Fri.*, *Sat.*, and *Sun.* On calendars, *M, T, W, T, F, S* and *S* is acceptable use.

4.10 Abbreviate *St.* in *St. Louis, St. Paul, St. Petersburg.* Abbreviate the mountain but spell the city: *Mt. Everest, Mount Vernon.* Abbreviate the army post name but spell the city: *Ft. Leavenworth, Fort Meyer.*

4.11 Spell out percent (one word) and use figures before it: *8 percent.*

4.12 Names of foreign countries are not abbreviated.

5. NUMBERS

5.1 In general text, spell out *one* through *nine* and use numerals for *10* and over: *one time, three days, 18 children, 50 years, 78 women, 200 delegates*.

5.2 Use numerals to state specific or technical measurements, dates, times of day and page numbers: *4x6 feet, 8 1/2x11-inch paper, 4 cubic feet, 92 degrees, 15 percent, 2,289 votes, 35mm film, 45-rpm record; July 14, 1993 or 14 July 1993; 6 p.m., 5:30 a.m.; page 5, pages 11-17.*

For casual statements of measure, i.e., of height, weight, length and volume, however, follow the general rule of writing out numbers under 10: *the room looked about eight feet wide; the page had one-inch margins; the pool was nine and one-half feet deep; a four-pound roast; five feet tall.*

5.3   When one numeral follows another, avoid confusion by alternating styles of usage or rewriting the sentence: *eleven 45-rpm records; one hundred 20-cent stamps (or 100 twenty-cent stamps); ten 4-foot boards, 200 fives.* Do not let one number stand next to another if there is any chance of confusion. Recast the sentence to avoid such a construction as: *Of the 324, 168 already have been obtained.*

5.4   When a number begins a sentence it must be spelled out. If the number is very long, rewrite the sentence to avoid opening with it.

5.5   Poetic and idiomatic numbers are spelled: *A thousand times no! I've told you a hundred times.*

5.6   Write out *million, billion and trillion: $1 million, $300 billion, $10 trillion, a million times.*
An exact amount can be written: *$4,251,756.*
The decimal is carried to two places: *$4.25 million.*

5.7   Ordinary sums of money follow the general rule: *nine dollars; 25 cents; a thirty-dollar hat; $10; a $250 donation; $650,000.*

5.8   When combinations of large and small numbers are used in one passage to refer to like subjects, use the rule for the larger numbers: *The group was made up of 7 children, 43 women, and 32 men; He paid $8 for his Hackysack; I paid $11 for mine.*

5.9   Use numerals for statistical material, tables and charts, and in numbers with decimals.

5.10   Use numerals for military units, political divisions, and court districts: *6th Fleet, 10th ward.*

6. GRAMMAR

Building a sentence is like building anything else. There are certain basic parts to work with. In English these parts, identified by their uses in the sentence, are:

Subjects, verbs, objects (direct, *d.o.*, and indirect, *i.o.*), modifiers (adverbs, *adv.*, and adjectives, *adj.*), and connectives such as "and" and "but."

These sentence parts are combined into units called phrases and clauses. Clauses have subjects and verbs. Phrases do not.

The number of clauses in a sentence and the relationship/s between and among the clauses determine basic sentence structure. The number of phrases does not affect the basic structure of a sentence.

The Simple Sentence

6.1   The basic English sentence is *one independent clause*. (A clause by definition has *a subject and a verb*.) An independent clause, as the name implies, stands alone. More often than not, the verb has a *direct object* or a *predicate adjective*.

> *Joe (s.) hit (v.) the wall(d.o.).*
> *I (s.) am (v.) lucky (p.a.).*

The simple sentence may consist of only two words— one subject and one verb:

> *Linda (s.) laughed. (v.)*
> *I (s.) erred. (v.)*

The simple sentence may have more than one subject:

> *Steve and Holly went surfing.*

It may have more than one verb:

> *They sang and danced all night.*

It may have both more than one subject and more than one verb:

> *Robin (s) and Ben (s.) worked (v.) all week and traveled(v.) all weekend.*

It may take more than one object:

> *George (s.) gave (v.) me (i.o.) a handsome book (d.o.).*
>
> *You (s.) can't judge (v.) a book (d.o.) or a film (d.o.) by its promotional hype.*

A simple sentence may consist of only one word—a verb with the subject understood.

> *See?* (Subject "you" and auxiliary verb "do" understood.)
>
> *Scat.* (Subject "you cat" understood.)

It can be very long if it carries a lot of baggage in modifiers. But no matter how many modifying words and phrases you hang on a simple sentence, its basic structure does not change as long as it has only *one clause:*

> *By the way, do not confuse* except—*meaning, as a verb,* to exclude *and, as a preposition,* excluding—*with* accept, *a verb meaning to receive a person gracefully or a situation with a combination of grace and resignation.*

This is a simple sentence because it has only one independent clause—*you (s.) confuse (v.)* The subject *you* is understood; *confuse* is the one verb; *except* and *accept* are words used as words and therefore noun objects; all the rest is modifying words and phrases.

The structure of the sentence changes when another clause is added. If the additional clause is dependent, the sentence is *complex*; if the additional clause is independent, the sentence is *compound*. If both dependent and independent clauses are added, the sentence is *compound-complex*.

The Complex Sentence

6.2 A complex sentence contains one *independent* clause and one or more *dependent* clauses—i.e., ones that cannot stand alone and that need an independent clause to lean on.

> *Do not say that you are "laying down" when what you are doing is lying down.*

Introductory adverb clauses that tell where, when, how or why require a comma after them:

> *After our work was done, we all ran to Seth's Pond.*

An adverb clause that follows an independent clause does not require a comma:

> *We all ran to Seth's Pond after our work was done.*
>
> *Smile when you say that.*

A *restrictive adjective clause* does not take commas:

> *This is the day that the Lord hath made.*
>
> *My neighbor who drives from Philadelphia to the island every week will be here tonight.*
>
> *The 18th century artist Catherine Lusurier lived in the family of the painters to King Louis XV.*

Nonrestrictive adjective clauses take commas:
> *My neighbor, who drives from Philadelphia to the island every week, will be here tonight.*

(If you have more than one neighbor, but only one who drives to the island every week, the phrase is a piece of essential information, and the commas are omitted. If you have only one neighbor, commas are used. But as there was more than one 18th century painter, it will never be right to use the phrase "The 18th century painter, Catherine Lusurier,..." or any similar phrase restrictively, i.e., with commas.)

These words usually mark the onset of a dependent clause:
> *after, although, as, as if, before, because, how, if, since, than, that, though, unless, until, what, when, where, whereas, whether, while, why, which, who, whom, whose.*

Can you tell which of these is a simple sentence, which complex?
> *1. At about noon, Lesley, Gay and I took Sophie and Cole across the great pond in the little motorboat to south beach, went crabbing and swimming for a while, and then just lay in the sun talking to some guys from New York.*
>
> *2. If you are so smart, why aren't you rich?*

(1. Simple: It has a compound subject (*Lesley, Gay and I*) and compound verbs (*took, went and lay.*) Everything else is a modifying word or phrase or a connective.
2. Complex: "*If you are so smart*" is a dependent clause with the subject "*you*" and the verb "*are*"; "*why aren't*

you rich" is the independent clause with the subject *"you,"* and the verb *"are."*)

A *dependent clause used alone* results in an error called a *fragment:*
> We will talk soon. When he can face the truth.

Correct this by making the dependent clause depend on the independent clause:
> We will talk as soon as he can face the truth.

or   We will talk when he can face the truth.

The Compound Sentence

6.3   The third basic sentence type is the compound sentence, which contains two or more independent clauses joined by the connectives *and, but, or, nor* or *for* used with a comma:
> Mrs. Hill harangued her for two hours, but Miss Evergood sat patiently throughout the ordeal.
>
> You wish to be forgetting me, but I don't wish to be forgotten. (—Samuel Johnson)

Two independent clauses joined with a semicolon also make a compound sentence:
> For hours Anne begged him to dance; finally Jock agreed.

To join two independent clauses with a comma and no connective is to commit an error called a *comma splice:*
> We waited at the airport for two hours, they were home all the time.
>
> We waited at the airport for two hours; they were home all the time. (correct)

But two very short independent clauses may be joined with a comma (see also 6.7):

> *He ran, I biked.*

> *We were home, we were happy.*

The Compound-Complex Sentence

6.4   The fourth sentence type is the *compound-complex* sentence, which contains two or more independent clauses and one or more dependent clauses.

> *We had waited behind the police barrier outside the U.N. for hours, but still I shouldn't have asked the riot police \ what they were to do\ if we crossed it.*

> *He walked and I ran \ until we arrived at the Golden Dragon.*

Common Errors in Sentence Structure

6.5   *Fragments.* A fragment is an incomplete construction. It usually results from mistaking a subordinate clause for a main clause or a verbal for a verb.

> *People parrot whatever they read. Thus failing to respect their own ability to think. Thus failing to seek the truth.* (fragments)

These fragments can be joined to the main clause in several ways to make a correct sentence with a finely tuned nuance of meaning:

> *People parrot whatever they read, thus failing to respect their own ability to think and to seek the truth.* (correct)

> *When people parrot whatever they read, they fail to respect their own ability to think; they fail to seek the truth.* (correct)

People who parrot whatever they read without thinking for themselves fail to respect their own ability to think and to seek the truth. (correct)

In the '60s, the choices in life seemed clear. The revolution or the million dollars. Freedom or security. (fragment)

In the '60s, the choices in life seemed clear: the revolution or the million dollars, freedom or security. (correct)

In the '80s it was hard to find people who thought of life at all. In terms of anything but money and celebrity. (fragment)

In the '80s it was hard to find people who thought of life in terms of anything but money and celebrity. (correct)

It was another sunny, happy day at Disney World. The real world seeming far away. (fragment: "seeming" is a verbal)

It was another sunny, happy day at Disney World, and the real world seemed far away. (correct: "seemed" is a verb)

6.6   *Fused sentences.* Failure to separate two independent clauses by connective or punctuation results in fused sentences.

I did not wish to appear ingenuous when he asked me how I live I used my son's ingenious line, "Mom is upper-crust homeless." (fused sentence)

I did not wish to appear ingenuous; therefore, when he asked me how I live, I used my son's ingenious line, "Mom is upper-crust homeless." (correct)

*We can't believe you did that what can you have
been thinking?* (fused sentence)

*We can't believe you did that. What can you
have been thinking?* (correct)

6.7   *Comma splice.* To join two main clauses with a comma
instead of a period or semicolon results in a comma
splice. Correct it by simply replacing the comma with a
semicolon or a period. If a period is used, capitalize the
word after it.

*His election could be a disaster for this country,
he has all the earmarks of a tyrant.* (comma
splice)

*His election could be a disaster for the country;
he has all the earmarks of a tyrant.* (correct)

*He talked longer than I thought anyone could talk
on one subject, it was stupefying, I thought I was
going to fall out of my chair.* (comma splices)

*He talked longer than I thought anyone could talk
on one subject. It was stupefying; I thought I was
going to fall out of my chair.* (correct)

A comma splice can be corrected in several other ways:
by adding a connective to coordinate the clauses or to
subordinate one clause to another, or by reordering the
sentence slightly. Any of these corrections also improves
the sentence by specifying the relationship between the
clauses:

*She says that I should be more interested in
popular culture, it is full of intelligence and
energy, I don't agree, it is banal and violent.*
(comma splices)

She says that I should be more interested in popular culture because it is full of intelligence and energy, but I don't agree; I find it banal and violent. (correct)

or   *but I find it banal and violent. In short, we disagree.*

National Health Care will cost a great deal of money, a great many people will benefit from it. (comma splice)

Although National Health care will cost a great deal of money, many people will benefit from it. (correct)

Two main clauses joined by a transitional connective (*consequently, however, moreover, nevertheless, therefore*) take a semicolon or a period between them:

I know he wants a constant companion, consequently I cannot marry him. (comma splice)

I know he wants a constant companion; consequently I cannot marry him. (correct)

Two or more short main clauses that are closely related may be properly joined by commas:

Sometimes we stumble, sometimes we fall.

I came, I saw, I conquered.

6.8   *Faulty parallelism.* The convention of parallelism is that in the interest of readability, elements serving the same purpose in a sentence should have the same "weight," the same grammatical structure. Thus, two or more items in a series are written in the same form: a phrase is followed by a phrase, a clause by a clause, a noun by a noun, a verb by a verb.

Failure to observe this convention results in a hodge-podge:

> As attorney general to the Cherokee Nation he found he had heavy responsibilities not only for the litigation of civil suits at the tribe level but also got involved in domestic disputes and even prosecuting a policeman who shot a Cherokee boy. (faulty)

> As attorney general to the Cherokee Nation, he found he had heavy responsibilities not only for the litigation of tribal civil suits but also for the resolution of domestic disputes and even for the prosecution of a policeman who shot a Cherokee boy. (correct)

6.9   *Dangling modifiers.* A dangling modifier is one that has nothing in the sentence to modify:

> By years of study in Vienna and Milan, his voice became a legend in operatic history.

(His voice did not study; he did. Thus "he" follows the modifying phrase:)

> By years of study in Vienna and Milan, he became a legend in operatic history.

> In order to be served, shirts and shoes must be worn.

(Shirts and shoes are not served, people are.)

> To be served, customers must wear shirts and shoes.

(Or, the admirably direct:) *No shirt, no shoes, no service.*

(The implied full thought is grammatically correct: Wear no shirt and no shoes, and get no service.)

When *only three years old, my mother went to war*. (dangling modifier)

When *I was only three years old, my mother went to war*. (correct)

6.10 *Shifts in subjects and verbs*. Awkward shifts in structure usually take one of two forms: shifts of subject (also called *person*) or shifts of verb tense within a sentence or paragraph.

When *you have seen enough murders with your lunch, a person is ready to give up the noon news*.

(Shift of subject from "you," which is *second person* to "a person," which is *third person*.)

When *you have seen enough murders with your lunch, you are ready to give up the noon news*. (correct)

I hated to turn him down, but you can't spend all weekend going to football games. (Two shifts: in subject from first person "I" to second person "you" and in verb tense from past "hated" to present "can't.")

I hated to turn him down, but I couldn't spend all weekend going to football games. (correct)

As the centuries passed, women's clothing becomes more and more abbreviated. (shift of verb tense from past to present)

As the centuries passed, women's clothing became more and more abbreviated. (correct)

6.11 *Incomplete constructions.* The omission of words necessary
for a clear understanding of the thought often results in
an ambiguous statement.

> *Statistics show that college women like their*
> *studies better than college men.* (ambiguous)

> *Statistics show that college women like their*
> *studies better than college men do.* (correct)

> *The colors this year are as bright, if not brighter*
> *than any fall I've seen here.* (ambiguous)

> *The colors this year are as bright, if not brighter*
> *than, the colors of any other fall I've seen here.*
> (correct)

Appendix 3

Formula Stories

FORMULAS STREAMLINE THE ROUTINE

Fresh writing marks good news stories. Imaginative reporters look for a way to write each story, one that captures what is unique in that story.

Readers tire of seeing the same kinds of stories written the same way time after time. Yet, the formula story has its place. Some stories just don't have enough to them to lend themselves to anything but routine treatment. They are not worth the time it would take to find an unusual way to write them. They will be read because of who or what is involved even if the news is not of great importance.

Stories of routine promotions and transfers of employees and stories about new policies are examples of this kind of story.

There is another reason for handling certain stories in a category the same way—it's democratic. It would be unfair, for example, to write a long detailed story about one employee's promotion, and a short, bare-bones story about the similar promotion of another employee. That's why newspapers often handle obituaries and wedding stories in a standard form, with exceptions for prominent or unusual people.

Beginning news writers learn by imitation. When they are assigned a story, they look for similar stories in the news. This not only gets them on the right track, but serves as a checklist to remind them of what should be included in the story. As they become more experienced and more confident, they seek new ways to write a story, ways to make it more inviting to the reader.

The following examples will serve as a guide for writing certain basic stories.

PERSONNEL ITEMS

The routine personnel item, such as a promotion or a transfer, should get right to the point:

Susan Lawrence has been promoted to Associate Director.

Lawrence, who joined the Arts Council three years ago as an executive assistant, was instrumental in the establishment of the Historic Preservation Council.

She received her bachelor's degree in art and architecture criticism from Harvard University in 1989 and is now studying for a master's degree in business at Berkeley.

In writing these stories, avoid such effusive expressions as: "Congratulations are in order to. . ." and "Hard work has paid off for. . ." Unless you are running a very chummy new operation, stick to the facts. Who got promoted to what? How long has she been with the organization? What did she do previously? What did she study at school?

There is a natural curiosity about new employees. In general news stories, however, avoid rambling on about matters that have no bearing on the story. New employee stories may legitimately report that the employee is married and has three children and served in Vietnam. But use feature material in feature stories.

MEETINGS

Many newsletter stories originate at meetings. It is not sufficient to start such a story by saying a meeting was held, that such-and-such was discussed and so-and-so attended it.

Find out what happened at the meeting. What was accomplished? What was said? Start with the most important result of the meeting:

Members of the Audubon Society are urged to form car pools as part of an effort to preserve air quality. A resolution adopted at the national board meeting last week called for all member chapters to join the effort to combat the number one cause of air pollution.

Jenkin David, board chairman, said that our efforts will...

The story would go on to list details of how car pools would be set up and operated. It would itemize other actions taken by the board, and it would give specific quotes and actions by individual society members or chapters.

If a meeting produces several results of nearly equal importance, the customary way to open the story is to summarize the action:

> *Funding for a $4 million interchange at I-72 and Robb Road, a $2 million improvement to the Green River sewage system, and a new $740,000 sanitary landfill was approved by the Roanoke Planning Commission last week.*
>
> *The interchange will connect highways 72 and...*

The story would go on to give details of each project, the background, what commission members had to say about the proposals, pro and con, and what the final vote was.

When a meeting produces no results, the reporter is sometimes hard pressed to find a news angle. Usually, there's something to be written:

> *After four hours of debate, the Spellman Community Hospital board voted to delay action on whether to seek federal funds for five new emergency medical vehicles until it could determine whether the hospital or the county would have responsibility for administering the expanded program...*

SPEECHES

Speech reporting follows the same pattern as reporting meetings. Single out the most important point the speaker made, document it in the paragraphs following the lead, then list other points made by the speaker:

> *There is no better way to prove the need for a regional council than to look at the metropolitan area from the air, according to Walt Bodine.*
>
> *Bodine, local broadcast-journalist and author, was principal speaker to more than 500 persons at the annual*

dinner meeting of the Mid-America Regional Council in late January.

"Go up in an airplane and fly over this great, sprawling community of ours," Bodine said. "Strain your eyes, but you won't see any state or county lines down below. From that lofty perspective, city limit signs are not very real."

Neighboring communities must work together to solve their problems, Bodine said. Those problems include. . .

If several points are to be stressed they can be combined in the lead, then documented in separate paragraphs following the lead:

New buses, expanded routes, more frequent service, and round-the-clock scheduling will all be needed to provide good mass transportation service to citizens of Dallas, Richard Davis, chairman of the Dallas Transit Authority, told regional transit officials last week.

In a speech, Davis called for...

First paragraph: (36 new buses)
Second paragraph: (41 more route miles of service)
Third paragraph: (14 maintenance and repair staff for a third shift)

Reports

Stories based on reports often start with the most important news and then itemize other elements of the report:

The 1994 Consolidated Electric general budget will be only one percent higher than the 1993 budget. The increase was kept reasonable by the skillful handling of...

Sometimes there are so many elements in a report that the lead will focus on the report itself, then go on to list the elements:

In a 105-page document, based on 2,500 pages of study, the Air Force has pictured the Kansas City area as it would be after nearly 4,000 military and civilian workers and their families leave Richards-Gebaur Air Force Base.

A draft Environmental Impact Statement compiled by the Air Force described the metropolis after the loss of population:

1. *The housing market is slack and money is tight.*
2. *Tax revenues drop and unemployment rises.*
3. *The quality of neighborhoods wanes, rates of vandalism and fires climb.*

If a report is deadly dull, chances are that quotes taken from the report will be dull, too. A good way to enliven a report story is to interview the person or persons who prepared it, seeking candid, straightforward quotes to brighten the copy.

NOTICES

A large number of stories are based on notices. They tell the reader that a specific action or event is scheduled at a certain hour, date and place. These stories take two basic forms:

The deadline for applications for New York Foundation for the Arts grants is June 30. Anyone who needs an application form may get one from the office, located at...

That's the direct approach. But often the reporter may want to interpret the importance of an event:

Students and faculty will have a chance to make their views known on the university's new merit pay policy at a hearing scheduled for next month.

The hearing will be held at Allen Hall, 2406 Olentangy Road on December 11 at 7:30 p.m.

Questionnaires will be circulated at the hearing. Participants will express their views in writing about whether the university should proceed with its plan to include student evaluation of faculty in the new policy.

A transcript of the hearing and a tabulation of the questionnaires will be made public before the plan goes to the state legislature for final action.

It is essential in notice stories to give the exact time, date and place an event is to be held.

After an event is held, however, the exact details as to time and place are no longer of primary importance and do not make a good lead.

On July 10, at 9 a.m., 400 employees of Hilton International gathered at Sailor Park for the annual picnic.

Start the story with some news from the picnic—the softball teams' scores or outstanding plays. Or treat such a story as a feature. If you want to use the date and location in the lead, generalize them (i.e., *last Saturday at Orient Park*). But in most cases it is wise to use these two now past w's—the when and the where—farther down in the story.

CONTROVERSIES

Many good stories involve controversy. There's nothing wrong with starting such a story with the word itself.

A controversy over how to finance a 911 emergency telephone system for the region has developed between Bell Telephone Company and Yellow River Regional Council.

Following the lead, give both sides of the controversy:

Fletcher White, vice president of the phone company, criticized the council's recent proposal to add a surcharge to customers' bills to pay for the system. He said it should be financed by some form of tax.

> *Richard Nesbitt, executive director of the council, said a tax was not feasible because so many different cities would be involved. Furthermore, he said, the cities are located in two different states, each with different enabling statutes for taxation.*

These are a few suggested approaches for writing certain kinds of stories often encountered.

There are many others, of course, and there is nothing wrong with a beginning reporter reading local newspapers and other newsletters for ideas of how to write stories.

But the eventual goal is to break away from formula writing and seek novel ways to tell some stories.

Appendix 4

Form
Contracts

VENDOR CONTRACT

This contract made this _____ day of _____, 199_,
between _____, the company, having an office at
_____ and the contractor, having an office
at _____.

WITNESSETH:

That in consideration of the agreements expressed herein, the
Company and the Contractor do hereby agree as follows:

ONE: The Contractor agrees to perform the following, hereinafter
referred to as "the work":

Set in type, print, and perform related activities necessary to
provide _____ copies per issue of the monthly publication,
_____ (name).

All work shall be done in a good and workmanlike manner and
to the satisfaction of the Company's representative.

TWO: The work to be performed shall be commenced and completed as follows:

Contract shall become effective on _____ and ter-
minate on _____. Company shall have the option to
renew this contract for two successive one-year terms upon the same
conditions as herein provided except as to "contract price" which
shall be mutually agreed upon at time of renewal. Company shall
exercise said option by notifying Contractor in writing at least 30
days prior to expiration of the initial term, or renewal term, as the
case may be.

THREE: Company shall pay to Contractor the following
_____ (state amount), hereinafter called the "contract
price." The sum to be paid to Contractor for the work includes any
and all local, state and federal taxes, charges, and excises that may
be imposed upon Contractor in connection with performance of
this Contract. Contractor expressly assumes and agrees to pay the

same. Final payment shall not be due and owing until 30 (thirty) days have elapsed after completion of the work and after compliance with the conditions of Provision Five.

FOUR: Company's representative is _____ (person designated by Company).

FIVE: Final payment shall be due and owing by Company after completion of all work, acceptance of work by Company, after receipt of the final bill and after the elapse of time stated in Provision Three. But Company may require Contractor to give evidence that all claims arising under the Contract have been satisfied and Contractor will reimburse Company for any money the latter may be compelled to pay for labor, material and other obligations.

SIX: Contractor shall be responsible for any material delivered to it by Company and shall return all material not required for completion of the work.

SEVEN: Contractor shall maintain complete and accurate records of labor, material and equipment. Company may inspect said records at all reasonable times.

EIGHT: The Company may reject any or all of the work if, in its opinion, same is not in accordance with this Contract. The Contractor shall repair or replace any rejected work within 24 hours after receiving written notice from the Company if notice is given during progress of the work. If notice is given following completion of the work, Contractor shall repair or replace any rejected work within seven days after receiving written notice.

NINE: Contractor shall not subcontract any part of the work without written consent of the Company.

TEN: Contractor shall have full control and direction over the mode and manner of performing the work.

ELEVEN: If, in the opinion of the Company's representative, the Contractor refuses or fails to supply a sufficient number of workmen, or the proper quantity or quality of material, or the necessary tools and equipment, or refuses or fails in any respect to carry on the work with promptness and diligence, the Company may give the Contractor written notice to remedy the default within 24 hours and, upon failure of the Contractor to remedy the default within such time, Company reserves the right to take over any or all labor, materials and appliances, to provide labor and material, and to complete or have completed any part or all of the work. The cost of completion by the Company shall be deducted from the unpaid balance, if any, due the Contractor under this Contract. If there is no unpaid balance, Contractor agrees to reimburse the Company for the cost of the completion.

TWELVE: Contractor expressly agrees not to discriminate against any employee or applicant for employment because of race, religion, sex or national origin.

IN WITNESS WHEREOF, Company and Contractor have executed this Contract in duplicate the day and year first above written.

_____

Company

_____

Contractor

PRINT PURCHASE AGREEMENT

your name & address here

Job #: _____

Representative: _____

Printer: _____

Address: _____

_____

Phone #: _____

Date Due: _____

Please note that failure to notify us of any delays 3 days prior to this due date will void this agreement.

Payment Terms: _____

Project Name: _____

❑ Mock-up included

❑ Confirmed price: _____

❑ Quantity*: _____ *This the minimum needed; underruns are not allowed and overruns not billable.

❑ Page size: ❑ 8 ½ x 11   ❑ 8 ½ x 14   ❑ 11x17   ❑ other: _____

❑ # Pages: ❑ front only   ❑ front & back   ❑ 4-page   ❑ ____ pages

❑ Fold   fold ____ times down to _____ (dimensions)

❑ Perforations: ____ as marked on mark-up copy

❑ Paper: ❑ weight: ___ ❑ name: _____ ❑ color: _____ ❑ finish: _____

❑ Ink Color: ❑ black   ❑ PMS #_____   ❑ PMS#_____   ❑ other: _____

❑ Photos: ❑ scanned in   ❑ need ____ halftones

❑ Screens: ❑ on artwork   ❑ need _____ cut

❑ Artwork: ❑ camera-ready: ❑ film   ❑ paper

        ❑ copy on disk, printer to typeset & layout

        ❑ layout on disk; printer to imageset

❑ Blue line or other proof required

❑ Press check required: Call _____ at _____ when ready for press.

❑ Packaging required: ❑ in boxes ready to ship   ❑ shrinkwrapped in ____ s

❑ Shipping: ❑ customer pick up   ❑ deliver to mailhouse at:

        ❑ deliver ____ samples to client at:

        ❑ deliver ____ samples to address above

        ❑ deliver balance to address above

❑ Ship via:

❑ Special instructions:

IMAGESETTING PURCHASE AGREEMENT

your name & address here

Job #: _____

Representative: _____

Date Due: _____

Service bureau: _____

Please note that failure to notify us of any delays 1 day prior to this due date will void this agreement.

Address: _____

_____

Phone #: _____

Payment Terms: _____

Project Name: _____

Contact: _____

❏ Storage medium: ❏ PC disk 3.5"   ❏ PC disk 5.25"   ❏ Mac disk

❏ Program used: _____ Version: _____

❏ Saved as EPS or other: _____

❏ File name(s): _____

❏ Mock-up included

❏ Typefaces used: _____

_____

❏ Linked artwork/files included on disk and noted on mock-up

❏ Confirmed price: _____

❏ Page size: ❏ 8 ½ x 11   ❏ 8 ½ x 14   ❏ 11x17   ❏ Custom: _____

❏ # Pages: _____

❏ Output: ❏ paper   ❏ resin coated (RC) paper   ❏ film

❏ Separations: ❏ 1-color   ❏ 2-color   ❏ 3-color   ❏ 4-color   ❏ other: _____

❏ Resolution: ❏ 600 dpi   ❏ 1200 dpi   ❏ 2,400 dpi   ❏ other: _____

❏ Line screen: ❏ 85   ❏ 110   ❏ 133   ❏ other: _____

❏ Delivery: ❏ call for pickup   ❏ send by courier

❏ ship via _____ to: _____

❏ Special instructions: _____

MAIL HOUSE PURCHASE AGREEMENT

your name & address here

Representative: _____

Mail House: _____

Address: _____

_____

Phone #: _____

Job #: _____

Date Due: _____

Please note that failure to notify us of any delays 2 days prior to this due date will void this agreement.

Payment Terms: _____

Project Name: _____

❑ Mock-up included

❑ Confirmed price: _____

❑ Quantity: _____

❑ Postage deposit of $_____ received by_____ (initials)

❑ Labels: ❑ peel & stick   ❑ Cheshire   ❑ to be output

❑ Zero-waste mailing (all names must be mailed)

❑ Fold: fold ____ times down to _____ (dimensions)

❑ Inspection of mailing required before shipped; call _____

❑ Remainders: ❑ customer pick up   ❑ deliver to us
              ❑ ship to: _____

              _____

❑ Special instructions:

Appendix 5

Resources for Editors

Books & Booklets on Newsletters

Editing Your Newsletter
by Mark Beach
Writer's Digest Books
1507 Dana Ave.
Cincinnati, OH 45207
(800)289-0963

Fundamentals of Successful Newsletters
by Thomas H. Bivins
NTC Publishing Group
4255 West Touhy
Lincolnwood, IL 60646-1975
(800) 323-4900

How to Create Powerful Newsletters
by Peggy Nelson
Bonus Books, Inc.
160 E. Illinois St.
Chicaco, IL 60611
(312) 467-0580

Making Money Writing Newsletters
by Elaine Floyd
Newsletter Resources
6614 Pernod Ave.
St. Louis, MO 63139
(800) 264-6305

Marketing With Newsletters
by Elaine Floyd
Newsletter Resources
6614 Pernod Ave.
St. Louis, MO 63139
(800) 264-6305

The Newsletter Sourcebook
by Mark Beach
North Light Books
1507 Dana Ave.
Cincinnati, OH 45207
(800)289-0963

Newsletters From the Desktop
by Joe Grossman
Ventana Press
P.O. Box 13964
Research Triangle Park, NC 27709
(919) 544-9404

101 Ways to Save Money on Newsletters
by Polly Pattison
Newsletter Resources
6614 Pernod Ave.
St. Louis, MO 63139
(800) 264-6305

Producing a First Class Newsletter
by Barbara Fanson
Self-Counsel Press
1704 N. State St.
Bellingham, WA 98225

Publishing Newsletters
by Howard Penn Hudson
(for subscription newsletters)
Newsletter Clearinghouse
P.O. Box 311
Rhinebeck, NY 12572
(914) 876-2081

**Quick & Easy Newsletters
on a Shoestring Budget**
by Elaine Floyd
Newsletter Resources
6614 Pernod Ave.
St. Louis, MO 63139
(800) 264-6305

Success in Newsletter Publishing
by Fred Goss
(for subscription newsletters)
Newsletter Publishers Association
1401 Wilson Blvd., Suite 207
Arlington, VA 22009
(703) 527-2333

Winning in Newsletters
(for subscription newsletters)
Newsletter Clearinghouse
P.O. Box 311
Rhinebeck, NY 12572
(914) 876-2081

**You CAN Sell Ads
in Your Newsletter**
Promotional Perspectives
1829 W. Stadium Blvd., Suite 101
Ann Arbor, MI 48103
(313) 994-0007

BOOKS ON DESIGN & TYPOGRAPHY

Editing by Design
by Jan V. White
R. R. Bowker
121 Chanlon Road
New Providence, NJ 07974
(908) 464-6800

**Desktop Publishing & Design
for Dummies**
by Roger Parker
IDG Books Worldwide, Inc.
919 E. Hillsdale Blvd., Suite 400
Foster City, CA 94404

**Editing the Organizational
Publication**
by Edmund Arnold
Ragan Communications
212 W. Superior St.
Chicago, IL 60605
(312) 335-0037

The Gray Book
by Michael Gosney
Ventana Press
P.O. Box 13964
Research Triangle Park, NC 27709
(919) 544-9404

Looking Good in Print
by Roger C. Parker
Ventana Press
P.O. Box 13964
Research Triangle Park, NC 27709
(919) 544-9404

Type & Layout
by Colin Wheildon
Strathmoor Press
2550 Ninth St., Suite 103
Berkeley, CA 94710-2516
(510) 843-8888

BOOKS ON PHOTOGRAPHY

**Photography for
Student Publications**
by Carl Vandermeulen
Middleberg Press
P.O. Box 166
Orange City, IA 51041
(712) 737-4198

**Photography for
the Graphic Designer**
by Norman Sanders
National Endowment for the Arts
1100 Pennsylvania Ave.
Washington, DC 20506
(202) 682-5400

Pictures for Organizations
by Phil Douglis
Lawrence Ragan Communications
212 W. Superior St.
Chicago, IL 60605
(312) 335-0037

**The World's Best & Easiest
Photography Book**
by Jerry Hughes
Phillips Lane Publishing
5521 Greenville Ave., Suite 104-732
Dallas, TX 75206

BOOKS ON INFORMATION GRAPHICS

Charts & Diagrams
by Nigel Holmes
Watson-Guptill
1515 Broadway
New York, NY 10037
(212) 764-7300

Information Illustration
by Dale Glasgow
Addison Wesley
1 Jacob Way
Reading, MA 01867
(617) 944-3700

Presentation of Data in Science
by Reynolds, Simmons
Kluwer Academic Publishers
101 Philip Assinippi Park
Norwell, MA 02061
(617) 871-6600

Using Charts & Graphs
by Jan V. White
R. R. Bowker
121 Chanlon Road
New Providence, NJ 07974
(908) 464-6800

BOOKS ON PRODUCTION

Getting It Printed
by Mark Beach
North Light Books
1507 Dana Ave.
Cincinatti, OH 45207
(800) 287-0963

Papers for Printing
by Mark Beach
North Light Books
1507 Dana Ave.
Cincinatti, OH 45207
(800) 287-0963

PUBLICATIONS ON DESIGN & EDITING

Before and After
PageLab
1830 Sierra Gardens Dr., Suite 30
Roseville, CA 95661
(916) 784-3880

The Board Report
P.O. Box 300789
Denver, CO 80203
(303) 839-9058

Communication Briefings
(1101 King St. Suite 110
Alexandria, VA 22314
(800) 888-2084

Editorial Eye
Editorial Experts
66 Canal Center Plaza, Suite 200
Alexandria, VA 22314-1538
(703) 683-0683

Editors Forum
P.O. Box 1806
Kansas City, MO 64141
(913) 236-9235

Editors Only
P.O. Box 430
Winstead, CT 06098

Inhouse Graphics
United Comm. Group
11300 Rockville Pike, Suite 11
Rockville, MD 20852-3050
(800) 929-4824
(301) 816-8950

Memo to Mailers
USPS NAIC
6060 Primacy Parkway, Suite 101
Memphis, TN 38188-0001

Newsletter Design
Newsletter Clearinghouse
P.O. Box 311
Rhinebeck, NY 12572
(914) 876-2081

Newsletter News & Resources
Newsletter Resources
6614 Pernod Ave.
St. Louis, MO 63139
(800) 264-6305

The Newsletter Newsletter
(for religious editors)
Communications Resources
P.O. Box 2625
North Canton, OH 44720
(216) 499-1950

Newsletter on Newsletters
Newsletter Clearinghouse
P.O. Box 311
Rhinebeck, NY 12572
(914) 876-2081

Newsletter Trends
Sterling Communications, Inc.
1920 Ellesmere Road, Suite 104
Scarborough, ON M1H 2W7
(416) 512-2218

The Page
P.O. Box 14493
Chicago, IL 60614

The Ragan Report
Ragan Communications
212 W. Superior St.
Chicago, IL 60605
(312) 335-0037

Step-By-Step Electronic Design
Dynamic Graphics
6000 N. Forest Park Drive
Peoria, IL 61614
(800) 255-8800

Type World
PennWell Publishing Co.
10 Tara Blvd., 5th Floor
Nashua, NH 03062-2801
(603) 891-0123

The Williams Report
Williams Communications, Inc.
P.O. Box 924
Bartlesville, OK 74005
(918) 336-2267

FILLERS FOR NEWSLETTERS

The CopyWriter
Narrative Strategies
13A Roberts Road
Cambridge, MA 02138
(617) 661-1839

Clip Edit
Dartnell Corp.
4660 N. Ravenswood Ave.
Chicago, IL 60640
(800) 621-5463

First Draft
Ragan Communications
212 W. Superior Street
Chicago, IL 60605
(312) 335-0037

Funny Fillers
The GROMA Corp.
565 Pearl St., Suite 200
La Jolla, CA 92037
(619) 454-6626

Ideas Unlimited
9700 Philadelphia Court
Lanham, MD 20706-4405
(800) 345-2611; (301) 731-5202

Pages
Berry Publishing
300 N. State St.
Chicago, IL 60610
(312) 222-9245

CLIP ART MANUFACTURERS

Art Pak Clip Art Services
1420 N. Claremont Blvd. #205D
Claremont, CA 91711
(909) 626-8065

Arts & Letters
15926 Midway Road
Dallas, TX 75244
(214) 661-8960

Church Art on Disk
Communication Resources
4150 Belden Village St.
Canton, OH 44718
(800) 992-2144

ClickArt
T/Maker Company
1390 Villa St.
Mountain View, CA 94041
(415) 962-0195

Cliptures
Dream Maker Software
925 W. Kenyon Ave., Suite 16
Englewood, CO 80110
(800) 876-5665

Creative Media Services
Phil Frank's Megatoons
P.O. Box 5955
Berkeley, CA 94706
(510) 843-3408

Designer's Club
Dynamic Graphics Inc.
6000 N. Forest Park Drive
Peoria, IL 61656-1901
(800) 255-8800

Dover Publications
Clip Art Series and Pictorial Archive
180 Varick St.
New York, NY 10014
(212) 255-3755

Formatt Art Series
Graphic Products Corp.
1480 South Wolf Road
Wheeling, IL 60090
(708) 537-9300

Gazelle Technologies Inc./EduCorp
7434 Trade St.
San Diego, CA 92121
(800) 843-9497; (619) 536-9999

Health Care P.R. Graphics
Solution Resources
1121 Oswego St. Suite 1
Liverpool, NY 13088
(800) 962-1353

Images With Impact
3G Graphics
114 Second Ave. S., Suite 104
Edmonds, WA 98020
(800) 456-0234

Publications Co.
1220 Maple Ave.
Los Angeles, CA 90015
(818) 991-8085

TechPool Studios
(medical electronic clip art)
1463 Warrensville Center Road
Cleveland, OH 44121
(216) 291-1922

CARTOONS

Cartoons by John's
P.O. Box 1300
Pebble Beach, CA 93953
(408) 649-0303

Comics Plus
(Syndicated Strips)
United Media
200 Park Ave. 6th Floor East
New York, NY 10166
(800) 221-4816

Creative Media Services
P.O. Box 5955
Berkeley, CA 94705
(510) 843-3408

Farcus Cartoons, Inc.
Box 30006, Station C
Ottawa, ON Canada K1Y 4J3
(613) 235-5944

Funny Business
EduCorp
7434 Trade St.
San Diego, CA 92121
(800) 843-9497; (619) 536-9999

Grantland Enterprises
(cartoons for organizations)
460 Bloomfield Ave., Suite 307
Montclair, NJ 07042
(201) 509-7688

NEWSLETTER DIRECTORIES

Hudson's Newsletter Directory
The Newsletter Clearinghouse
P.O. Box 311
Rhinebeck, NY 12972
(914) 876-2081

Newsletters Directory
Gale Research Co.
835 Penobscot Blvd.
Detroit, MI 48226
(313) 961-2242

Oxbridge Directory of Newsletters
Oxbridge Communications
150 Fifth Ave., Ste. 302
New York, NY 10011
(212) 741-0231

**The Monthly Catalog
of US Government Publications,
The Monthly Checklist
of State Publications**
Dept. of Documents
US Government Printing Office
Washington, DC 20402

Ulrich's Intl. Periodicals Directory
R.R. Bowker
121 Chanlon Road
New Providence, NJ 07974
(908) 464-6800

PROFESSIONAL ASSOCIATIONS

American Corporate Identity
4100 Executive Park Drive
Cincinnati, OH 45241

Am. Medical Writers Association
95650 Rockville Pike
Bethesda, MD 20816
(301) 493-0003

Am. Society of Assoc. Executives
(1575 Eye St. NW
Washington, DC 20005
(202) 626-2723

Art Directors Club
250 Park Avenue S.
New York, NY 10003
(212) 674-0500

Assoc. Business Writers of Am.
1450 S. Havana, Suite 424
Aurora, CO 80012
(303) 751-7844

Catholic Press Association
3555 Veterans Highway Unit O
Ronkonkoma, NY 11779-7636
(516) 471-4730

**Council for Advance & Support
of Education (CASE)**
11 Dupont Circle
Washington, DC 20036
(202) 328-5900

Education Writers Association
1331 8th St. NW
Washington, DC 20036
(202) 637-9700

Health Care Marketing Division
American Marketing Assoc.
(has a communication section)
250 S. Wacker Drive #200
Chicago, IL 60601
(312) 658-0536

Hispanic Public Relations Asso.
1 Technology Drive, Suite C515
Irvine, CA 92718
(714) 453-0116

**International Association
of Business Communicators**
One Halladie Place, Suite 600
San Francisco, CA 94102
(415) 433-3400

Ntl. Assoc. of Desktop Publishers
462 Old Boston St.
Topfield, MA 01983
(508) 887-7900

National Association of Realtors
11th St. NE, Suite 200
Washington, DC 20001
(202) 383-1000

Newsletter Publishers Association
1401 Wilson Blvd. #207
Arlington, VA 22209
(703) 527-2333

Printing Industries of America
100 Dangerfield Road
Alexandria, VA 22314
(703) 519-8100

**Society of National Association
Publications (SNAP)**
1650 Tysons Blvd., Suite 200
McLean, VA 22102
(703) 506-3285

Society of Newspaper Designers
The Newspaper Center
P.O. Box 4075
Reston, VA 22090
(703) 620-1083

Society of Professional Journalists
P.O. Box 77
Greencastle, IN 46135
(317) 653-3333

Society of Publication Designers
60 East 42nd St. #1130
New York, NY 10165
(212) 983-8585

Soc. of Technical Communication
901 N. Stuart St., Suite 904
Arlington, VA 22203-1821
(703) 522-4114

Type Directors Club
545 W. 45th St.
New York, NY 10036
(212) 983-6042

Writers Connection
P.O. Box 24770
San Jose, CA 95154
(408) 445-3600

WRITER'S REFERENCES

**American National Standard Proof
Corrections**
ANS Institute
New York, NY
Contains all the proofmarks.

Headlines and Deadlines
by Robert E. Garst
& Theodore M. Bernstein
Columbia University Press
New York, NY

Manual For Writers, 5th Edition
by Kate Turabian
University of Chicago Press
Chicago, IL

**Proofreading & Editing
for Word Processors**
by Sheryl Lindell
Arco
New York, NY

The Writer's Market
Writer's Digest Books
1507 Dana Ave.
Cincinnati, OH 45207
(800)289-0963

Writing Fast While Writing Well
by David Fryxell
Writer's Digest Books
1507 Dana Ave.
Cincinnati, OH 45207

Newsletter Seminars

Editorial Experts
66 Canal Center Plaza, Suite 200
Alexandria, VA 22314
(703) 683-0683

**How to Create Newsletters
People Will Read**
Padgett-Thompson
11221 Roe Ave.
Leawood, KS 66211
(800) 255-4141; (913) 451-2900

Newsletter Design
Dynamic Graphics Ed. Fndn.
6000 N. Forest Park Drive
Peoria, IL 61614
(800) 255-8800; (309) 688-8866

**Producing, Designing & Writing
Newsletters**
Newsletter Factory
Bldg. 8, Suite 110
1640 Powers Ferry Rd.
Marietta, GA 30067
(404) 955-2002

Promotional Perspectives
1829 W. Stadium Blvd., Suite 101
Ann Arbor, MI 48103
(313) 994-0007

Publication Design
Pattison Productions
5092 Kingscross Road
Westminster, CA 92683
(714) 894-8143

Ragan Communications
212 W. Superior St.
Chicago, IL 60605
(312) 335-0037

Writing & Interviewing Seminars

Advanced Writing & Interviewing
Thomas Hunter
Effective Communications Group
309 Windsor Terrace
Ridgewood, NJ 07450
(201) 444-3147

CALENDAR MAKING SOFTWARE

CalendarMaker
CE Software, Inc.
P.O. Box 65580
W. Des Moines, IA 50265
(515) 224-1995

CREATIVITY SOFTWARE

IdeaFisher Software
IdeaFisher Systems, Inc.
2222 Martin St., Suite 110
Irvine, CA 92715
(800) 289-4332; (714) 474-8111

TYPEFACE LIBRARIES

Adobe Type Libraries
Adobe Systems, Inc.
P.O. Box 7900
Mountain View, CA 94039
(800) 833-6687; (415) 961-4400

ONLINE RESEARCH

America Online
8619 Westwood Center Drive
Vienna, VA 22182
(800) 827-6364

CompuServe
P.O. Box 20212
5000 Arlington Centre Blvd.
Columbus, OH 43220
(800) 635-6225

Dialog Information Services, Inc.
3460 Hillview Ave.
Palo Alto, CA 94304
(800) 334-2564

Dow Jones News/Retrieval Service
P.O. Box 300
Princeton, NJ 08543
(609) 520-4000

Mead Data Central
P.O. Box 933
Dayton, OH 45401
(513) 865-6800

Prodigy
445 Hamilton Ave.
White Plains, NY 10601
(800) 776-3449

Index

A

abbreviations, 73-74, 98
acronyms, 77
active voice, 76, 96
addresses, verifying, 75
adjectives, 76, 97
Adobe Photoshop, 157
Adobe Type Collection, 115
adverbs, 86
advertising, 10
advertising agencies, 31
advocacy, 49-51
Alexander, Shana, 74
alliterations, 96, 99
alphabet-and-a-half, 128
alumni publications, 46
America Online, 22, 174
announcements, 40, 119
annual reports, 16-17, 43
articles (see *stories*)
artists (see *graphic artists*)
artwork (see *illustrations*)
ascenders, 118-119
Associated Press, 158
Associated Press Stylebook, 73
associations, 3, 9, 10, 13, 15-17, 22, 39
attribution, 72, 76, 98
audiences, 9-10, 13, 15-17, 39, 45-46, 116
auto leading, 130
awards, 48

B

back-up copy, 30
banks, 10, 14
Bernstein, Theodore M., 9, 99
bids, 32, 167
board members, 16, 31-34, 43, 42
body copy, 140
    reversing, 138, 140
    typefaces for, 114, 117-120

bold italic, 117
boldface, 117, 122
book reviews, 4
borders, 159
bosses (see also *management*), 21, 31-34
    interviewing, 56
boxes, 109, 121, 159
broadsheets, 10
brochure, 10
bromides, 77
budget (see *costs*)
bulk rate mailings, 169-170
bulleted lists, 133
bulletin boards, 47, 71
businesses (see *company news*)

C

calendars, 13
cameras, 152
capitalization, 73, 122, 149
captions, 103, 107, 117
cartoons, 44
celebrities, 57, 70
changes, 32-33, 87-88
charities (see *non-profit organizations*)
chronological form, 82
church newsletter, 9-10
circulation, 36, 168
circumlocutions, 76-77
cities, 10
city directories, 75, 89
civic efforts, 45
clichés, 77
clip art, 159
clippings (see *news clips*)
club newsletter, 9-10
colors
    four-color, 9
    of ink, 15
    of paper, 168
    of type, 138

column inches, 135
columns
    number of, 113, 124-128, 135
    space between, 128-129, 131
    specifying, 149
comics, 44
commas, in headlines, 99
community, sense of, 13, 15, 17, 39, 43
company news, 3, 9, 17
comprehension, reading, 113
CompuServe, 22, 174
computers, 34, 103, 173-174
conclusions, of articles, 73, 81
condensed typefaces, 119, 136
conferences, 55
content, 9-10, 14, 16, 22
    appropriate, 45-51
    approval of, 32-34
    ideas for, 28, 39-47
    for electronic newsletters, 173-174
    for external newsletters, 49
    for internal newsletters, 46-49
    selecting, 55
    sizing up, 87
contents box, 109
continuing articles, 138
contractors (see also *vendors*), 41
contracts, vendor, 31
contributors, 22-24, 33, 103
controversies, 61, 63, 74
conventions, 17, 39
copy editing, 86-89
copyfitting, 99, 134, 136-138
copyright law, 63-65
corrections, 60
costs, 13, 30-36
    of book reviews, 44
    of printing, 114, 167-168
counting words (see *word counts*)
credibility, 50, 60, 73
criticism, 61
cropping photographs, 156
customers, 10, 13-14, 39
    content for, 49
    interviewing, 56
    profiles of, 42
cutlines, 107, 117

D

daily news, 124
dates, 4
deadlines, 29, 30, 32, 167
decks, 103, 105, 122
defaults (see *desktop publishing, defaults*)
delayed lead, 72, 79-81
descenders, 118-119
design, 22, 30
    culprits, 138-141
    effects of editing on, 86, 103-109
    and text, 113
desktop publishers, 21, 24
desktop publishing, 21, 30, 113
    cost of, 35
    defaults, 114, 129-134
    software, 34, 124
    systems, 113
    typefaces for, 114-115
    type sizes on, 116
dictionaries, 75, 78, 89
direct lead, 79-80
disk, computer, 29, 31, 34, 60
distributing, 10, 168
doctors, 16
donors, 23, 39
draft, rough or first, 85
drop caps, 159
dumb quotes, 105
dummy, 145-147, 167

E

editing, 10
editors
    and copy editing, 86-89
    job definition of, 10, 21-36
    as designers, 135
    of newspapers, 86
editorial schedules, 27
editorials, 43, 55, 121
electronic formats, 31
electronic mail, 13, 16, 22, 29, 85
electronic publishing
        (see *desktop publishing*)
employees, 10, 14-16, 33
    distributing to, 168
    profiles of, 42, 46

entrepreneurs, 9-10, 15
equipment, 30-31, 34-36
Eras, 120
errors, 60
events, 4
exclamation points, 98-99
executives (see *management*)
external newsletters, 16, 23, 33

F

facing pages, 146
facts, checking, 75-76
fair comment, 63
family news, 28, 47
fax messages, 13, 16, 22, 29, 85
fax-on-demand systems, 173-174
features
    definition of, 45
    headlines of, 121
    leads of, 81
    material for, 47
    writing style of, 55, 70-72
Federal Register, 41
figure legends, 117
filing system, 60-61
First Amendment, 62
first class mailings, 169
fliers, 13
flush left, 137
format, 9-10
Franklin Gothic, 120
freedom of speech, 62
freelancers, 31
frequency, 9, 16
fund raising, 23

G

Garamond, 120
Garst, Robert E., 99
glossy paper, 113-114
goals (see also *mission*), 13-14, 23, 31
gossip (see *rumors*)
Goudy Old Style, 117
government agencies, 10, 15, 32, 41
Government Printing Office (see *U.S. Government Printing Office*)

government statistics, 29
grammar (see also *proofreading*)
    checking, 88
    standards for, 73, 75
graphic artists, 21, 24, 30-31
graphics (see *illustrations*)
graphs, 83
grids (see also *columns*), 124, 127
guest columns, 43
Gutenberg, 163

H

hammerheads, 122
Harris, Jean, 74
headline schedules, 122-123, 137
headlines, 9, 93-99
    attracting attention with, 94-95
    in electronic newsletters, 173-174
    placement of, 141, 147
    punctuation in, 98-99, 138
    puns in, 93
    of standing columns, 44
    styles for, 24, 95-96
    typefaces of, 114-115, 120-124
    verbs in, 93
    words for, 99
Headlines & Deadlines, 99
Helvetica, 118, 120
history, 43, 70
homework (see *research*)
Hornschuch, Jerome, 163
hospitals, 14-16, 39, 43
human interest stories, 70
human resources department, 40
hyphenation, 124, 133
hyphenation zone, 133

I

illustrations, 10, 15, 135-136
image, 14-15, 17, 33, 113-114
inches, 129
indents, 133, 149
index, 148
indicia, 170
information graphics, 83
initial caps, 159

inquiring photographer, 43
instructions, 24
insurance companies, 10, 16, 39
internal newsletters, 16, 23, 33, 40, 44-49
international news, 41
Internet, 22, 173-174
interviews, 42-43, 55-59
    questions for, 57-58
    as sources of news, 55
    by telephone, 56
    writing up, 72-73
inverted pyramid form, 82
investment firm, 15
invitations, 119
italic type, 117, 121, 139

J

jargon, 39
journalism training, 22, 93-94
jump headlines, 148
jump lines, 148
jumps, 148
justified margins, 132, 139

K

kerning, 134
kickers, 103, 105, 107, 122
Kiplinger (see *Washington Kiplinger Letter*)
Kiwanis Club, 40

L

label heads, 95, 105
labels, for mailing, 168-169
lawsuits, 63
layout, 10, 24
    dummying, 145
    effects of editing on, 86-87, 103-109
    of inverted pyramid articles, 82
    of short shorts, 82
leadership, 21-36
leading, 130, 134, 138, 140
leads, 9, 29
    delayed, 72, 79-81
    direct, 79-80
    hidden, 87

length of, 103
    use of quotes in, 72-73
    rewriting, 87
    writing, 69, 78-81, 85
lectures, 17
legal problems, avoiding, 62-64, 78
legibility, of type, 113-114
letter-sized newsletters (see *newsletters, letter style*)
letter spacing, 134
letters, 4, 13
    from the president, 33, 44, 97-98
    to the editor, 44
libel, law of, 62-63
line length, 128
Linotronic, 30

M

magazines, 10, 28, 122
mailing, through post office, 169
mailing indicia, 135
mailing lists, 168
mailing service, 21
mailing space, 135
malice, 63
management, 10, 23, 31-34
    editorials from, 43
    profiles of, 42
    of publication by editor, 21-36
margins, 128, 132, 135
mass media, 13, 17
masthead, 114, 135, 145
meetings, 13, 17, 39-40, 55
members, 10, 13-15, 17, 33
    interviewing, 56
memos, 40, 47, 60, 71
messages from president (see *letters from president*)
minutes, 40
mission, 14-15, 23
modem, 29
modern type, 117
morale, 14, 23
    of employees, 47-49
    of volunteers, 24, 28
mug shots, 107, 155

N

nameplates, 135, 145
names, verifying, 75
National Geographic, 158
networks, 13
New York Times, 9, 39, 93
New York World Tribune, 118
New Yorker, 42
news clips, 58, 60, 75
news pegs, 70-71
news releases, 17
news thread, 83
newsletters
    letter-style, 4, 114
    definition of, 9-10, 103
newspapers, 3, 9-10
    daily, 71, 85
    experience writing, 85
    headlines in, 93, 122
    reporters for, 50
    school, 4, 9
newsprint, 113-114
non-profit organizations, 39, 41
note taking, 58-59, 78-79, 85
numbers
    making charts with, 83
    in headlines, 99
    in lists, 133
    spelling out, 73
    standards for, 73

O

old style type, 117
online services, 173-174
opinion columns, 43-44

P

page numbers, 109
page sizes (see *sizes*)
PageMaker, 129, 131
pages, number of, 9
Palatino, 120
paper, 10, 15, 113-114, 167-168
paperless publishing, 173-174

paragraphs
    breaking up long, 87
    indenting, 133
    length of, 76, 103
paraphrasing, 72-73
passive voice, 76, 96
parents, 28
Pattison, Polly, 108
Pattison's Principles for Pull Quotes, 108
periods
    in headlines, 99, 138
    spacing after, 103
permits, postal, 169-170
Philadelphia Bulletin, 93
photo illustrations, 158
photo montages, 158
photographers, 21-24, 30-31
photographs, 30
    captions for, 107
    cost of, 35
    editing, 158
    filing, 60-61
    and headlines, 97
    layout of, 135-136, 145-147
    scanned, 34, 60-61, 157-158
    selecting, 152-155
    sizing, 136, 157
    styles for, 24
physical therapists, 41
picas, 116, 129, 133
pie charts, 83
politicians, 43
points, 116, 129
points-times-two rule, 128
positive construction, 97
postal regulations, 169-170
present tense, 97
printing, 30
    collecting bids, 167
    cost of, 35, 167
    saving on, 167-168
Prodigy, 22, 174
productivity, increasing, 47-49
proofreading
    checklist, 165
    with computers, 88, 164
    while editing, 86-89
    help with, 89, 163

proofreading (cont.)
  history of, 163-164
  marks, 166
  tips for, 163-166
preferences, 129
press releases, 40, 44, 60
printers, 21, 24, 30, 114
privacy, right of, 63
public figures, 63
public relations, 17, 31
publicity duties, 22
publication guidelines, 31
pull quotes, 103, 108
punctuation
  checking, 86
  in headlines, 98-99
  standards for, 73
puns, 93, 96, 99
purpose (see also *mission*), 14-15
puzzles, 4

Q

qualifiers, 86
question heads, 95
questions, for interviews, 57-58
quotation marks, 99, 105
quotes
  in captions, 107
  detail through, 40
  enlivening through, 56
  from experts, 41
  in leads, 72-73
  shorthand for taking, 59
  use in article, 72

R

ragged right margins, 132, 139
RAM, 34
readability, 113-142
readers (see *audience*)
recognition, 48
recycled paper, 114
regulations, government, 41
releases, copyright, 63-65
reporter form, 25, 28
reporters, 21-30, 39
  of newspapers, 50

reporting, 55-64
  news, 69
reports, 40, 56, 60
reprints, of articles, 43-44, 64-65
research, 55-64, 85
research findings, 40
resources, 21
retractions, 63
reversed type, 124, 138-140
rewriting
  first drafts, 85
  of leads, 87
rhymes, 96, 99
roman type, 117, 120
rules, 121, 131
rumors, 48-51, 57, 61

S

safety, 45
sales, 13, 45
sans serif type, 117-120
scaling photographs, 157
scaling type, 136
scanners (see also *photographs, scanned*), 34
Scarsdale diet, 74
schedules, 24
  project, 26
  yearly editorial, 27
scholar's margin, 125
school newsletter (see also *newspaper, school*), 9-10
screens, 138-139, 159
script typefaces, 119
search and replace function, 103
second class mailings, 169
secondary headlines, 121
sentences
  length of, 76
series, 42
serif type, 117-120
shield laws, 64
short shorts, 81-82, 121
side issues, 80
sidebars, 83-84
sizes, of newsletters, 10, 15, 114, 129
sizes, of type (see *type sizes*)
small caps, 122

smart quotes, 105
solos, 148
sources, of news, 55-64
soy-based ink, 114
speeches, 17, 40, 55-56
spelling (see also *proofreading*)
  checking, 86, 88
  of names, 75
  standards for, 73
  trouble with, 74-75
sports scores, 46
spreads, 146
staff, 21
stamps, 170
standing heads, 105, 114, 145
statistics, 40, 83
Stone Sans Serif, 120
Stone Serif, 120
stories, (see also *content*), 10, 14, 22, 24
  continuing, 148
  length of, 103, 106
  number per page, 103
  placement of, 145-147
straight news, 69, 81
stringers, 22, 28-30, 39
structured form, 82-83
style guide, 24, 103
stylebooks
  checking with, 86, 89
  definition of, 73
  headline schedules, 122-123
  model, 73, 78
stylesheet, 74
subheads
  and design, 103, 122
  type styles for, 106
  usage, 87, 106
subscription newsletters, 10, 15, 17
suspense
  in body copy, 82-83
  in leads, 80-81
support, 14
synonyms, 97-99

T

table of contents (see *contents boxes*)
tabs, 133

tape recorders, 59
Tarnower, Herman, 74
team, newsletter, 21-31
teasers
  in captions, 107
  in contents boxes, 109
  in leads, 80
  on mailing panel, 109
telephone books, 75, 89
telephone calls, 13
telephone numbers, 4
television, 13
thesaurus, 78
third class mailings, 169-170
time (that a newsletter takes), 13
time element, 70-72
times, of events, 4
Times Roman, 120
titles, 73
tracking, 134
training
  of editors, 35
  of volunteers, 28-30, 36
transcribing notes, 59
Type & Layout, 138
type sizes
  of body copy, 116, 119
  copyfitting by changing, 134, 136
  of headlines, 94, 116, 119-123
  and leading, 130
  specifying, 149
  standard, 120-123
type styles
  choices of, 117
  of headlines, 94, 120-123
  specifying, 149
  standard, 120-123
typefaces
  of body copy, 34, 117-120
  of captions, 107
  of headlines, 34, 94
  of pull quotes, 108
  selecting, 10
  of typed newsletters, 113
typesetting (see *desktop publishing*)
typesetting specifications, 151
typewritten newsletters, xi, 36, 124

U

underlining, 117, 124
unions, 10
U.S. Government Printing Office, 64
University of Chicago Stylebook, 73
unjustified margins, 132, 139
uploading, 173

V

vendors, 21, 24
  minority, 32
  union, 32
verbs, in headlines, 99
volunteers, 3, 14, 23-30, 39
  editors, 49
  profiles of, 42

W

Washington Kiplinger Letter, 4, 114, 124
Washington Post, The, 93
weather forecasts, 46
Webster's New World Dictionary, 75
weight, of paper, 113, 167-168
Winners & Sinners, 9
white papers, 40
word counts, 24, 28, 33, 85, 103, 135-137
word processors, 59, 103, 114, 124-125, 136
word spacing, 124
WordPerfect, 131
works for hire, 64, 66
world almanac, 89
World Wide Web, 173
wrapping type, 133
Writer's Market, 44
writers, 21, 23-24
writing, 9-10
  features, 70-72
  interviews, 72-73
  leads, 78-81
  news, 28, 69, 82-83
  short shorts, 81-82
  speeding up, 85
  style, 15, 28-29, 69-73
  tone of, 47-49

X

x-height, 118-119

About the Authors

Marvin Arth has degrees in law and journalism. He has reported, edited and directed news for major newspapers and television stations in Cincinnati, Kansas City, San Francisco, Washington D.C. and New York. He has taught journalism at the University of Kansas and conducted newsletter workshops nationally. Arth is a former editor of *The Washington Business Journal*.

Helen Ashmore has a master's degree in English and has taught writing at the universities of Kansas, Missouri, Hawaii and Northern Colorado. She has been an editor for Hallmark Cards and for *American Family Physician* magazine and has directed public relations programs for public and private organizations.

Elaine Floyd owns and operates Newsletter Resources in St. Louis, Missouri. She's the author of *Marketing With Newsletters, Quick & Easy Newsletters on a Shoestring Budget, Making Money Writing Newsletters* and *Advertising From the Desktop*.

She currently edits a subscription newsletter, *Newsletter News & Resources*, and trains newsletter editors internationally.

Colophon

This book has been set in Goudy Old Style, a remarkably handsome, versatile and readable typeface designed by Frederic W. Goudy in 1915. It achieves its grace, warmth and soft sparkle by the slight curving of many strokes and the subtle styling of serifs.

The photographs shown in Chapter 10 are from the Professional Photography Collection from DiscImagery and the Kids Collection from Gazelle Technologies. Both are available from EduCorp, 7434 Trade St., San Diego, CA 92121; (800) 843-9497; (619) 536-9999.

Free Copy of Newsletter News & Resources

Call, write or fax for your free copy of the most recent issue of *Newsletter News & Resources*.

Every issue includes new products for newsletter editors, design tips and trends, how to streamline production and control costs, reports on new technology for printing, layout and the Internet, and real-life examples of internal and external newsletters.

Photocopy and send this form. Please do not remove this page from the book. Doing this will damage the special lay-flat binding.

Name: _____

Title: _____

Company: _____

Address: _____

City/State/Zip: _____

Phone: (_____) _____

Do you use Windows, DOS or Mac? _____

Are you currently doing a newsletter? _____

Software used? _____

Do you have a CD-ROM? _____

☎ (314) 647-0400   **Fax** (314) 647-1609

✉ Newsletter Resources
6614 Pernod Ave.
St. Louis, MO 63139